The Random House Book of

Plants for

Shade

ROGER PHILLIPS
& MARTYN RIX

Research by Anne Thatcher
Design by Jill Bryan & Debby Curry

RANDOM HOUSE

Acknowledgements

We would like to thank the following gardens and
suppliers for allowing us to visit them and
photograph their plants:
The Royal Horticultural Society's Garden, Wisley;
The Royal Botanic Gardens, Kew; PepsiCo Gardens,
Purchase, New York; Ann and Roger Bowden;
Brooklyn Botanic garden, The Hillier Arboretum;
Eccleston Square Gardens; Washfield Nurseries;
Sandling Park; Tintinhull House, Somerset;
Hatfield House, Hertfordshire.

Among others who have helped in one
way or another we would like to thank:
Marilyn Inglis, Gill Stokoe
and Alison Rix

 BB FR AN C EA OP

Random House website address:
www.atrandom.com

Printed in Great Britain
98765432
First U.S. Edition

Color Reproduction by Aylesbury Studios Ltd.
Printed by Butler and Tanner Ltd. Frome, Somerset

Contents

Introduction......................................4
Early Spring Perennials......................6
Early Spring Bulbs...........................10
Early Spring Shrubs.........................14
Spring Perennials............................18
Spring Bulbs...................................36
Spring Shrubs.................................40
Summer Perennials..........................56
Summer Bulbs.................................80
Summer Shrubs...............................82
Autumn Shrubs & Bulbs...................90
Evergreen Shrubs............................92
Index..94

Brunnera and Dicentra growing in shade at the PepsiCo Gardens, New York, USA

if one is aware of its restrictions and chooses plants accordingly.

The Text

We have kept the language of the text simple, explaining any complicated terms as we go along. Common names are given in Roman print, Latin names in italics; synonyms (syn(s).) – other names for the same plant – are given in brackets. Plants are categorized as either evergreen or deciduous, the overall size is noted, together with dimensions of flowers and leaves. Hardiness, in farenheit, centigrade and US zones is given, and we have specified the origin of the plant, sometimes describing the native habitat in more detail.

Planting Help

Each individual plant or group of plants is further illuminated by a section called Planting Help which gives hints on planting, propagation, pests and diseases.

Introduction

There are many different types of shade and an immense diversity of possible plants for individual requirements. This book is arranged roughly in flowering order, ending with examples of autumn colour, although we have kept groups of bulbs, shrubs and perennials together.

Many shrubs and spring-flowering bulbs grow well under deciduous trees before the leaves appear; early-flowering bulbs, which provide a reliable and intense display of colour, are happy grown in places that are covered by perennials in summer. Patches of vivid colour can be produced by shade-tolerant annuals and earlier by spring-flowering perennials. Foliage variety is important in any garden and certainly cannot be ignored in a shade garden where variegation creates stunning results.

It is important to define the limitations of the shaded area in question: is it dry or boggy; is it shaded only at certain times of the year; what is the soil like? Even the most hopelessly shaded area can be transformed,

Soil

Soil can be either heavy with a high proportion of clay, or light with a high proportion of sand or fine gravel. Soil can be either humus-rich, comprising peat and dark soils, or humus-poor comprising sand, chalk or clay derived from subsoil; most soils benefit from the addition of humus. Another important factor is whether the soil is acid, neutral or alkaline; neutral or slightly alkaline soils may be made more acid by the addition of sulphur.

Planting

When planting shrubs and perennials, prepare the soil in advance by digging in organic matter, preferably leaf mould or rotted garden compost. After planting and watering, mulch with 1–2in (2.5–5cm) of weed-free, organic matter. Leaf mould, leaves, bracken, coarse peat, bark chippings or even old newspapers covered with soil will help to prevent weeds and retain moisture. Liberal feeding with liquid fertilizer in spring after planting will ensure strong plants. Nowadays, shrubs are usually bought in pots and it is essential to soak them in water for an hour before planting if in loam, or overnight if in soil or peat.

As a general rule, bulbs should be planted when dormant. Plant in early autumn for spring-flowering bulbs, or in early spring for summer-flowering ones; to their own depth in heavy soil and twice or more than their own depth in light or dry soil. Soil fertility is unimportant if bulbs are planted for bedding and then discarded. However, if they are planted permanently or retained for future use, it is essential that the soil is fertile. Apply bone meal, chrysanthemum or rose fertilizer before planting or sprinkle on the surface immediately after planting.

Propagation

Seed Some seeds require a cold period to induce germination; some do not germinate in the first or even the second year after planting. Seedlings are best potted as soon as possible, so they make good growth before their first winter.

Cuttings Hardwood cuttings should be about 1ft (30cm) long and a small part of the bark should be scratched away at the base, or have a heel of the old wood. Place in sand or compost outdoors or in a shady frame in autumn – both shoots and roots should begin to grow in spring.

Take softwood cuttings as soon as the wood has begun to harden; too soon and the shoot will collapse, too late and the shoot is woody and will not form roots easily. Mist propagation has proved the greatest help in rooting softwood cuttings, and mist combined with bottom heat and the right degree of shading will induce many of the most difficult subjects, such as deciduous azaleas, to root.

Division Most perennials are easily propagated by division of the clumps; in spring in wet climates or in autumn in climates where spring and summer are rather dry. Dig up the clumps and either break apart by hand, or force apart by inserting two forks back to back and lever the clump apart.

A daffodil, hyacinth or allium can be induced to form bulblets by making a cross in the base of the bulb and inserting a small stone to keep the sides apart. Few-scaled bulbs, such as fritillaries, can easily be increased by breaking the scales apart and planting each separately. In many-scaled bulbs, such as lilies, single scales can be broken off and planted in loose peaty soil with the tip just above the surface. Corms are more difficult; crocuses can be induced to make more than one shoot by cutting out the single main shoot, stimulating production of buds on the edge of the corm. Tubers and rhizomes can sometimes be increased by cutting them into pieces, depending on the number of growing points. Tuberous roots will often make new plants if divided at their point of attachment.

Soldiers and Sailors *Pulmonaria officinalis*

Pests & Diseases

The healthier the plant, the less likely it is to suffer from pests and diseases; a balanced supply of humus will usually ensure trouble-free gardening. Snails and slugs may be kept at bay by surrounding plants with a layer of grit, and a jar of old beer will also reduce their numbers. Surround bulbs with a layer of coarse sand when planting to keep small mammals from eating the bulbs.

The Hosta garden of Ann and Roger Bowden in Devon

Hellebores

Lenten Rose

Christmas Rose *Helleborus niger*

Stinking Hellebore *Helleborus foetidus*

Helleborus purpurascens

The Hellebore is one of the most delightful flowers of winter and early spring, easy to grow and producing large numbers of seeds. These evergreen plants flourish in moist, reasonably well-drained fertile soil in sun or partial shade; they are good under tall deciduous trees or in the shadow of a north-facing wall. The flowers are long-lasting and the leaves provide attractive ground-cover. Most Hellebores are herbaceous, although *H. corsicus*, *H. foetidus*, *H. lividus* and their hybrids produce leafy stems one year and flowers the next, before dying to make way for new shoots. Hellebores provide an attractive foil for many other shrubs and perennials, and the sheer range of possible colour varieties enables any aspiring garden designer to achieve perfect visual harmony in an otherwise uninspired bed!

PLANTING HELP   Before planting, prepare the soil by digging in some organic matter. Place individual plants in holes about 18in (45cm) across, lined with planting mixture. Ensure that they are not too close together, leaving enough space between the plants to grow other shade-loving plants, such as primroses and anemones. Hellebores vary in their speed of growth but once established are generally trouble-free, needing little attention throughout the year, although regular mulching can be beneficial. It can be fun to develop some of the little seedings that inevitably spring up around existing plants; the variety of colours produced is surprising! Alternatively, hellebores can be propagated by division.

Corsican Hellebore *Helleborus argutifolius* (syns. *H. corsicus*, *H. lividus* subsp. *corsicus*)   Valuable for foliage and flowers alike, this plant produces flowers 1½in (4cm) wide from January to April. Usually reaching about 2ft (60cm) tall and wider, the plant is short-lived but self-seeding; if seeds are not required, cut down stems after flowering to prevent black spot. Hardy to 0°F (−18°C), US zones 7–10. Native to Corsica and Sardinia.

Stinking Hellebore *Helleborus foetidus*
The foliage, bracts and flowers of this plant are impressive from autumn to late spring. Growing to 2½ft (75cm) tall and 4ft (1.2m) wide, it bears flowers ¾in (2cm) across from January to April, but the foliage has a rather unpleasant smell when broken. Short-lived but self-seeding; black spot can be a problem. Hardy to −10°F (−23°C), US zones 6–9. Native to western Europe and especially tolerant of dry shade. The form 'Wester Flisk' has a good purple flush on the stems and greyish leaves.

Christmas Rose *Helleborus niger* Probably the showiest of the wild Hellebores, producing flowers 1½–3in (4–8cm) across from January to April; these are pink-backed or turn pink as they age. Stems 9–12in (23–30cm). Cultivation is not always easy; a rich limy soil in partial shade, a good moisture supply and protection from slugs will facilitate success.
Hardy to −30°F (−35°C), US zones 4–8. Native to pine woods in mountains of central Europe.

Lenten Rose
Helleborus orientalis
Flowering from early January, this species grows to 18in (45cm) tall and produces flowers 2–3in (5–8cm) across. Numerous cultivars, from white to almost black, have been selected, some with contrasting nectaries and different degrees of spotting and aspect of flower. Some seedling strains illustrated here are:
'Atrorubens', 'Celadon' and 'Cosmos'. Hardy below 0°F (−18°C), US zones 7–10, although leaves can be killed by cold winds below 15°F (−10°C). Native to E Europe and Turkey.

'Atrorubens'

'Celadon'

Helleborus purpurascens Probably the hardiest of the species, flowering from mid-December to April, this variety can reach 12in (30cm) tall, producing flowers 1½–2in (4–5cm) across. The two most common colour varieties are purple with green interior and dark bluish purple with a similar but paler interior. Leaves deciduous. Hardy to −10°F (−23°C), US zones 6–9. Native to eastern Europe.

Corsican Hellebore *Helleborus argutifolius*

Lenten Rose *H. orientalis* at Washfield Nurseries

Helleborus orientalis 'Cosmos'

Lesser Periwinkle *Vinca minor*

Vinca minor 'Argenteovariegata'

Vinca difformis in SE Spain

Periwinkle

The foliage of periwinkle or vinca excels as effective ground-cover for shady areas and provides an excellent foil for other plants. Fast-growing and easily propagated, Vincas will quickly cover a bare patch of earth, but they can become invasive. These evergreen sub-shrubs and herbaceous perennials, native to woodland areas, are grown for their simple, attractive, often variegated leaves, while their singly borne star-like flowers add interest.

Lesser Periwinkle *Vinca minor*

PLANTING HELP Plant periwinkle in autumn or spring in any soil in sun or shade; mulch in autumn and early spring until well established. Propagate by digging up and moving naturally rooted stems. Alternatively, take semi-ripe cuttings in early summer or hard-wood cuttings in winter, and root in soil-based compost in a cold frame. No pruning is necessary but in order to contain vincas it is a good idea to cut them back fairly hard in spring after flowering, using either shears or a powered strimmer. Rust can be a problem, especially on *Vinca major*, but they are relatively free of pests and diseases.

Vinca difformis This plant forms mounds of evergreen stems 3½ft (1m) tall, bearing leaves 1–2½in (2.5–6cm) long, and producing pale blue to almost white flowers 1in (2.5cm) across from March to April. Tolerant of dry shade. Hardy to 10°F (−12°C), US zones 8–10. Native to SW Europe and North Africa.

Lesser Periwinkle, *Vinca minor* An evergreen forming mats of creeping and rooting stems to 6in (15cm) tall, bearing leaves ½–1¾in (1.5–4.5cm) long, and producing flowers 1in (2.5cm) across from February to June. Easily grown in sun or partial shade. Hardy to −10°F (−23°C), US zones 6–9. Native to SW and C Europe. There are numerous variants differing in flower colour, doubleness and leaf variegation. Shown here are:
Vinca minor **'Atropurpurea'** (syn. 'Purpurea Rubra') Dark plum purple flowers.
Vinca minor 'Azurea Flore Pleno' (syn. 'Caerulea Plena') Double sky blue flowers.
Vinca minor **'Argenteovariegata'** (syn. 'Variegata')
Silver-edged leaves and small mauve flowers about 1in (2.5cm) across produced in spring. Variegated leaf forms such as this tend to be less vigorous.

Vinca minor 'Atropurpurea'

Dead Nettle

***Lamium* species** The 50 or 30 different types of *Lamium*, usually perennial but sometimes annual, come from a wide range of habitats in Europe, Asia and North Africa. Groups of two-lipped flowers carried on spikes are produced from late spring to summer. However, they are grown mainly for their attractive foliage and excellent ground-covering capacity, although the larger species can sometimes be invasive.

Lamium maculatum 'Roseum'

PLANTING HELP Plant in autumn or early spring in moist, well-drained soil in dense or partial shade. To prevent unwanted invasion, dig up and separate rhizomes (underground horizonal creeping stems) in autumn or early spring; these can either be replanted elsewhere or discarded. Plants will need tidying up in late winter. Slugs and snails can be a nuisance.

Lamium maculatum An herbaceous perennial that grows to 8in (20cm) tall with creeping and rooting stems forming mats of heart-shaped, bright green leaves, striped or mottled with white. In spring and early summer it produces purplish hooded flowers 1in (2.5cm) long, in clusters on erect stems. Partial shade. Hardy to −30°F (−35°C), US zones 4–8. Native to much of Europe and W Asia. **'Roseum'** has pink flowers, **'White Nancy'** has white flowers and silver leaves.

Lamium galeobdolon 'Florentinum' (syns. *Galeobdolon luteum, Lamium galeobdolon* 'Variegatum') Yellow Archangel Grows to 24in (60cm) tall, bearing spikes of brown spotted flowers to ¾in (2cm) long from April to June.

Very invasive, with variegated leaves to 2½in (6cm) long. Hardy to 0°F (−18°C), US zones 7–10. Native to Europe from Ireland east to European Russia and south to Spain.

Bugle

Ajuga reptans A creeping evergreen perennial that grows up to 6in (15cm) tall and much wider spread; useful for ground-cover in dry shade. It produces erect spikes with several small deep blue flowers, rarely pink or white, up to ¾in (2cm) in spring. The oval or oblong leaves are up to 1½in (4cm) long; there are different forms with varying leaf shapes and colours. Hardy to −10°F (−23°C), US zones 6–9. Native to most of Europe, North Africa, W Asia and naturalized in North America. Valued for centuries for healing wounds, some claim it is useful for hangovers; its tea is reputedly good for soothing an irritable cough.

PLANTING HELP Plant in autumn or early spring in any soil, in shade or partial shade.

Wild Bugle *Ajuga reptans*

Lamium maculatum 'White Nancy'

Lamium galeobdolon 'Florentinum'

Glory of the Snow *Chionodoxa*

Winter Aconite *Eranthis hyemalis*

Snowdrop

Galanthus nivalis The small bulbs of snowdrops will form a clump 5in (12cm) tall, producing delicate, scented white flowers in January and February. They prefer partial shade but will grow in full sun. Hardy to –30°F (–35°C), US zones 4–8. Native to woods of W Asia and the Mediterranean and naturalized in much of northern Europe, providing a welcome display of beauty in the heart of the bleak winter landscape.

PLANTING HELP
Plant snowdrops in partial shade immediately after purchase in moisture-retentive, humus-rich, well-drained soil, 3in (8cm) apart to a depth of 3in (8cm). A top-dressing of bonemeal each autumn will improve flowering results. Depending on the quality of the soil, Snowdrops can spread to cover large areas; they prefer heavy soils like clay and humus-rich sand. Propagate by dividing clumps of bulbs as soon as the flowers begin to die down.

Snowdrop
Galanthus nivalis

Winter Aconite

Eranthis hyemalis   Grows to 2–3in (5–8cm) tall and 2in (5cm) wide, forming clumps that produce bright yellow flowers 2–3in (5–8cm) across, framed by bright green leaves in late winter and early spring. Winter aconites look wonderful under deciduous trees where they form great masses of flowers in late winter and early spring. They are easy to grow and will establish themselves into large colonies, particularly in alkaline soil. This plant is particularly good under Horse Chestnut trees. Hardy to 0°F (−18°C), US zones 7–10. Native to France, Italy, the former Yugoslavia, Bulgaria and Turkey but widely naturalized elsewhere.

PLANTING HELP   Plant tubers 2in (5cm) deep in moist, fertile, humus-rich soil in autumn; be careful the tubers do not become too dry before planting as they can be difficult to grow. Propagate by separating tubers with a spade in spring after flowering. Slugs may eat the foliage.

Glory of the Snow

Chionodoxa **species**   Easy to grow in sun or partial shade, this plant grows to 6in (15cm) tall and flowers in January and February, increasing rapidly. Hardy to −10°F (−23°C), US zones 6–9. Native to the Mediterranean region and W Asia.

PLANTING HELP   Plant bulbs in late summer or early autumn to a depth of about 3in (8cm) in moist but well-drained soil 2in (5cm) apart. A sandy chalky soil is preferred and a mulch of fine rich compost in winter will encourage vigorous bloom. To ensure maximum health, it is a good idea to lift, divide and replant these bulbs every five years or so.

Snowdrop *Galanthus nivalis* growing through a carpet of ivy.

Cyclamen coum

Celandine *Ranunculus ficaria*

Ranunculus ficaria 'Brazen Hussy'

Cyclamen

Cyclamen coum (syns. *C. atkinsii*, *C. orbiculatum*)
This bulb produces pink flowers about ¾in (2cm)
long in early spring. Hardy to 0°F (−18°C), US
zones 7–10. Native to the E Mediterranean region
and to W Asia.

PLANTING HELP   Plant 2in (5cm) deep in
moderately fertile, humus-rich, well-drained soil
in partial shade under trees or shrubs, and mulch
annually with leaf mould. Mice or squirrels
sometimes dig up the bulbs.

Iris

***Iris* 'Katharine Hodgkin'** (*Iris histrioides* ×
I. winogradowii)   This beautiful little iris grows to
4in (10cm) tall and produces flowers 3in (8cm)
across in early spring. The leaves are small and
insignificant at flowering time but elongate later.
Hardy to −30°F (−35°C), US zones 4–8. This
hybrid was raised in 1958 by E. B. Anderson and
named after the wife of Eliot Hodgkin, a great
grower of bulbs in Berkshire, England.

PLANTING HELP   Best planted in autumn in
well-drained, slightly limy soil in a sunny position.

Celandine

Ranunculus ficaria An attractive plant for
damp shady places in a wild part of the garden.
Some weed forms spread very quickly and can be
invasive. Grows to 2in (5cm) tall, producing shiny
yellow flowers ¾–1¼in (2–3cm) across from
January to May and bearing leaves up to 2in (5cm)
long. Hardy to 0°F (−18°C), US zones 7–10.
Native to Europe eastwards into C Asia.
Ranunculus ficaria **'Brazen Hussy'**
Has flowers with shiny golden petals, brown
underneath and glossy, dark brown leaves, often
bronze as seedlings.

PLANTING HELP   Plant in moist soil with
plenty of humus and propagate by dividing tubers
immediately after flowering, or in autumn. Slugs,
snails, aphids and mildew can cause problems.

Iris 'Katharine Hodgkin'

Wood Anemone

Windflower
Anemone nemorosa
A creeping perennial
with stems up to
6in (15cm) long,
producing solitary flowers
1in (2.5cm) wide, emerging
with the young leaves in
early spring. The flowers
are usually white with
some pinkish-purple on
the outside of the
petals, but may be
pink or even blue,
especially as they fade.
Pollinated by beetles, flies
and bees attracted by the
pollen. The plant disappears
in early summer, surviving by
means of the its underground rhizomes.
Hardy to 0°F (−18°C), US zones 7–10. Native to
N Europe, eastwards to Turkey and NW Asia,
growing in woods and on shady hillsides,
sometimes also on sea cliffs or heathy
mountainsides. Also in places which may have
been wooded in the past, but have certainly been
open for many hundreds of years.

Wood Anemone

PLANTING HELP   Plant in moist, fertile soil
in autumn in partial shade. Sow seed in containers
when ripe or divide in spring. Caterpillars, slugs
and small weevils may attack the leaves.

Wood Anemone *Anemone nemorosa*

Correa
'Mannii'

Viburnum × *bodnantense*
'Dawn'

Correa

***Correa* 'Mannii'** (syn. *C.* 'Harrisii')
An evergreen shrub that grows to 3ft (90cm) tall
and usually wider, producing tubular red flowers
about 1¼in (3cm) long, intermittently from
December to April. The oval leaves to 1in (2.5cm)
long, smell pleasant when bruised. Hardy to 20°F
(–6°C), US zones 9–10. A hybrid between two
Australian shrubs, *C. pulchella* and *C. reflexa*.
Raised in Australia in the 19th century.

PLANTING HELP   Plant correas in early
autumn or late spring. No regular pruning
required other than cutting away damaged shoots.
Free from pests and diseases. Good for a dry
sunny position under tall deciduous trees.

Viburnum

***Viburnum* × *bodnantense*
'Dawn'**   This easily cultivated
deciduous shrub grows to 10ft (3m)
tall and bears compact clusters of
small strongly scented, funnel-shaped
pink and white flowers ½in (1.5cm)
long, opening from red buds in late
winter. The leaves are 5in (12cm) long.

PLANTING HELP   Plant viburnums in
autumn or spring in any soil, in sun or shade.
Hardy to –10°F (–23°C), US zones 6–9. No
regular pruning is required and this shrub is
seldom affected by pests and diseases. *Viburnum*
× *bodnantense* is a hybrid raised in Wales in the
early 20th century.

Mahonia × *media* 'Charity' with *Echium pininana* against a background of bamboo in Eccleston Square

Mahonias

An evergreen genus of about 70 species originating in the woods of Asia, Central and North America. Thriving in full or partial shade, Mahonias can enhance a gloomy area of the garden throughout the year with their handsome foliage and attractive flowers and fruits. The low-growing species, such as *Mahonia aquifolium*, provide excellent ground-cover and the taller species, such as *Mahonia × media* 'Charity', will add interest and elegance to any garden. Some of the Asiatic species with fragrant flowers are less tolerant of cold.

PLANTING HELP   Plant mahonias in moist, reasonably fertile, well-drained soil with plenty of humus. Mahonias will perform much better in a deep rich loam. Place seeds in a seedbed or container in autumn and root leaf-bud cuttings from late summer to autumn. Any unwanted or damaged shoots can be cut back lightly after flowering in spring to retain the shape of the bush. Generally unaffected by pests and diseases, but rust and mildew can be a problem, especially on *Mahonia aquifolium*.

Mahonia × media 'Charity'

Oregon Grape *Mahonia aquifolium*   A suckering shrub that grows to 3½ft (1m) tall and eventually wider, bearing glossy leaves to 10in (25cm) long and producing clusters of bright yellow flowers ½in (1.5cm) wide in early spring. The fruit is a blue black berry. Tolerates deep shade. Hardy to 0°F (−18°C), US zones 7–10 or lower. Native to W North America where it grows in conifer forests. Especially useful for dry shaded areas.

Mahonia japonica   Grows to 5ft (1.5m) tall with several main stems from ground level. In winter it produces a profusion of arching spikes to 8in (20cm) long or more with very sweetly scented, pale yellow flowers ½in (1.5cm) wide. The leaves, borne in a cluster towards the tip of each branch and often copper tinted when young, are 1–1½ft (30–45cm) long. The fruit is a blue black berry. Hardy to 0°F (−18°C), US zones 7–10. Native to China and long cultivated in Japan.

Mahonia × media 'Charity'   An easily grown tall variety, reaching up to 10ft (3m) tall with several main stems from ground level, eventually making a bush wider than tall. In late autumn and winter it produces many spikes 10in (25cm) long or more, of slightly scented, bright yellow flowers ½in (1.5cm) wide, in a cluster towards the tip of each branch. The fruit is a blue black berry. Hardy to 0°F (−18°C), US zones 7–10. *Mahonia × media* 'Charity' is a hybrid between *M. japonica* and *M. lomariifolia*. 'Charity' was raised in the UK in the mid-20th century.

Oregon Grape

Oregon Grape *Mahonia aquifolium*

Mahonia japonica

Daphnes

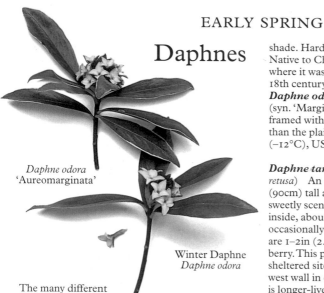

Daphne odora
'Aureomarginata'

Winter Daphne
Daphne odora

The many different
species of Daphnes
which grow wild in woodlands and on
mountainsides in Europe, N Africa and
subtropical Asia, vary in size, shape and flower
colour. They can be deciduous or evergreen and
are generally grown for their fragrant flowers,
foliage and fruit. Be careful if you have children
though; the berries are highly toxic if eaten and the
sap can irritate skin.

PLANTING HELP   Daphnes thrive best in
moderate shade, although some varieties, such as
D. laureola (*right*) and *D. pontica* (*not shown*) will do
well in dense shade. Plant in moist, rich, well-
drained soil in autumn or early spring; mulch in
autumn and fertilize in spring. Propagate by
division in autumn or early spring. No pruning is
necessary, but old woody shoots may be cut back
after flowering. Generally free from serious pests
and diseases, although aphids and leaf spot can
sometimes affect Daphnes.

Spurge Laurel *Daphne laureola*   A bushy
evergreen shrub that grows to 3½ft (1m) tall and
as wide, producing small, sweetly scented yellow
flowers in late winter, followed by round black
fruits. Glossy dark green leaves 3in (8cm) long.
Tolerates deep shade. Hardy to −10°F (−23°C),
US zones 6–9. Native to Europe and N Africa.

Winter Daphne *Daphne odora*   An evergreen
that grows to 3½ft (1m) tall and wide, producing
clusters of deliciously scented flowers about ½in
(1.5cm) long. Flowers are white inside but red or
deep pink on the outside, and are produced over a
long period in late winter. Leaves are 1½–3in
(4–8cm) long and the fruit is a black berry. Partial

shade. Hardy to 20°F (−6°C), US zones 9–10.
Native to China but long cultivated in Japan from
where it was introduced into cultivation in the
18th century.
Daphne odora 'Aureomarginata'
(syn. 'Marginata')   The dark green leaves are
framed with a very narrow cream margin. Hardier
than the plain-leaved *Daphne odora*, to 10°F
(−12°C), US zones 8–10.

Daphne tangutica Retusa group (syn. *D.
retusa*)   An evergreen shrub that grows to 3ft
(90cm) tall and wider, producing dense clusters of
sweetly scented reddish-purple flowers with white
inside, about ⅓in (1cm) long in late spring and
occasionally in autumn. The purple tinged leaves
are 1–2in (2.5–5cm) long and the fruit is a red
berry. This plant benefits from a
sheltered site by a south or
west wall in cooler areas, and
is longer-lived than some
Daphnes. Partial shade.
Hardy to −10°F (−23°C),
US zones 6–9. Native to
W China and introduced
into cultivation at the
beginning of the 20th
century by E. H. Wilson.

Daphne tangutica
Retusa group

Spurge Laurel *Daphne laureola*, wild in Kent

Hamamelis ×
intermedia 'Arnold
Promise'

Witch Hazel

There are five different types of witch hazel, a deciduous shrub that grow wild in and around woodlands and on riverbanks in E Asia and North America. Its autumn colour and fragrant frost-resistant flowers make it one of the most valuable of the winter-flowering shrubs.

PLANTING HELP   Plant in autumn or early spring in acid or neutral soil, rich in leaf mould, in sun or light shade such as in open woodland. Young plants have a tendency to grow in a sprawling fashion with no strong leading shoot, and it is therefore worth selecting a strong shoot to train upwards to give the bush some height. Thereafter remove any untidy branches in early spring. When ready, seeds can be collected and planted outdoors but will not come true; alternatively, cuttings can be taken from the plant in summer after flowering. Generally free from pests and diseases.

Hamamelis × *intermedia* **'Arnold Promise'**
Grows to 20ft (6m) tall and wider, producing yellow scented flowers about 1in (2.5cm) wide in winter on leafless branches, bearing leaves that turn shades of red or orange and yellow in the autumn. The fruit is a woody capsule about ½in (1.5cm) long, but is not ornamental. Hardy to

−20°F (−29°C), US zones 5–9. The hybrid witch hazels are the result of crossing the Japanese and Chinese witch hazels. This hybrid was first described from the Arnold Arboretum in Boston, USA. There are other cultivars in a selection of colours from pale yellow to deep red.

Hamamelis × *intermedia* **'Jelena'**   Produces a flower about 1in (2.5cm) wide that is red at the base, grading to orange-yellow at the tip, possibly the best form for autumn colour.

Chinese Witch Hazel *Hamamelis mollis*
Sometimes flowers as early as Christmas, this shrub merits a prominent position near a path where the wonderful scent can be enjoyed. Grows to 20ft (6m) tall and wider, producing rich yellow flowers 1in (2.5cm) wide on leafless branches, and bearing leaves that usually turn yellow in the autumn before falling. The fruit is a woody capsule about ½in (1cm) long but is not an ornamental feature. Hardy to −20°F (−29°C), US zones 5–9. Native to W China and introduced into cultivation in the late 19th century.

Hamamelis × *intermedia* 'Jelena'

Chinese Witch Hazel

Chinese Witch Hazel *Hamamelis mollis*

Bergenia cordifolia

Bergenia

This plant forms large patches of leathery leaves, it flowers in early spring and provides excellent ground-cover, tolerating even dry and windy conditions. Additional interest is provided by the dying leaves that sometimes become purple or scarlet. Many hybrids have been raised in gardens; they are hardy long-lived plants with evergreen leaves turning red or purple in the winter. Flowers open in early spring, but can be damaged by late frosts. All are hardy to −10°F (−23°C) or less and need a cool sheltered position in good soil.

PLANTING HELP   Bergenias like shade or partial shade and are best planted in rich, moist, well-drained soil mixed with humus. However, poor soil can encourage a more interesting leaf colour in winter. Bergenias do produce seeds but these do not always grow exactly like the parent plants. Rooted rhizomes of one or more leaf rosettes can be separated from the group and replanted elsewhere. It is a good idea to divide the clumps every three years or so to maintain healthy plants. Bergenias are susceptible to some pests and diseases, especially slugs.

Bergenia cordifolia   Grows to 18in (45cm) tall and wider, bearing veined leaves 8 × 12in (20 × 30cm) that remain green in winter. Dense heads of pale pink flowers ¾in (2cm) long, are produced from February to March. Native to Siberia. Introduced in the 17th century and very tolerant of cold and heat, growing well in shady places in Mediterranean climates. Hardy to −40°F (−40°C), US zones 3–8.

Bergenia 'Baby Doll'   Growing to 12in (30cm) tall and up to twice as wide, this hybrid bears bronze-tinted green leaves 4in (10cm) long, and produces pink flowers which darken with age in mid- to late spring. Hardy to 0°F (−18°C), US zones 7–10.

Bergenia 'Bressingham White'   Grows to 18in (30cm) tall and wider, bearing leaves 5in (12cm) long; producing dense heads of white flowers ¼in (0.5cm) wide in spring. Hardy to −10°F (−23°C), US zones 5–9. A hybrid raised in the UK in the 20th century.

Bergenia 'Bressingham White'

Bergenia 'Baby Doll'

Anemone rivularis

Anemone flaccida growing with *Corydalis flexuosa* in woods in Baoxing, Sichuan, China

Rue Anemone *Anemonella thalictroides* f. *rosea*

Anemones

Although most anemones need sun, some prefer moist, boggy shade.

PLANTING HELP   Both anemones illustrated here require moisture and shade and can be raised from seed. They may be affected by leaf spot, slugs and minute black weevils.

Anemone rivularis prefers humus-rich soil and tolerates drier conditions when dormant; this Anemone should be divided while in this dormant state. *Anemone flaccida*, on the other hand, thrives in peat and should be propagated in spring or autumn. It dies down soon after flowering.

Anemone flaccida   A modest but attractive plant for a woodland garden, this species forms clumps of stems 6–12in (15–30cm) long, bearing one to three white sometimes pinkish flowers ½–1in (1.5–2.5cm) across in late spring. Hardy to −10°F (−23°C), US zones 6–19. Native to Siberia, China and Japan, growing in shady places in ravines in loose peaty soil and on the banks of woodland streams.

Anemone rivularis   A clump-forming perennial that grows to 2ft (60cm) tall, bearing groups of flowering stems, producing white flowers with blue anthers and blue exterior, ½–1in (1.5–2.5cm) across in late spring. Hardy to −10°F (−23°C), US zones 6–19. Native to N India, Kashmir, Tibet and SW China in meadows, forest clearings, between rice fields and in hedges.

Rue Anemone

Anemonella thalictroides f. rosea (pink form) A delicate plant, slow to become established but which eventually spreads to form colonies. Delicate stems to 8in (20cm) long, producing pink flowers to 1in (2.5cm) across from spring to early summer. The leaves appear after the flowering stems. Hardy to 0°F (−18°C), US zones 7–10. Native of E North America, growing in damp deciduous and mixed woods.

PLANTING HELP   For a moist, loose, leafy soil in shade or partial shade. Sow seeds when ripe or propagate by division in spring. Slugs can make short work of this expensive plant!

Comfrey

Caucasian
Comfrey

Comfrey grows wild in damp shady
places, particularly near rivers and streams. It has
a thick, fleshy, branched root up to 1ft (30cm) or
more long, black on the outside, white inside, and
a hairy branched stem that grows 1–4ft
(30–120cm). Bell-shaped flowers grow in
drooping clusters and can be blue, purple, pink,
cream or white, blooming from April to October.
Comfrey has been valued for its medicinal
properties for centuries and modern research has
shown that it contains two substances, allantoin
and choline, which promote the healthy growth of
red blood corpuscles – vital after excessive loss of
blood from wounds or injuries.

Caucasian Comfrey *Symphytum caucasicum*
It produces sprawling stems to 3½ft (1m), bearing
alternate leaves and bright blue flowers to 1in
(2.5cm) long from April to July. For shade or
partial shade. Spreading rapidly, this plant will
smother anything except the largest perennials,
but is very pretty for a long season, flowering again
in late summer if the old stems are cut down.
Hardy to 0°F (–18°C), US zones 7–10. Native to
the Caucasus, growing in waste places, by streams,
in scrub and on grassy roadsides.

White Comfrey *Symphytum orientale*   Stems to
2¼ft (70cm) tall, producing white flowers up to
¾in (2cm) long from April to June. Tolerant of dry
shade if the soil is heavy. Hardy to –0°F (–18°C),
US zones 7–10. Native to SW Asia, growing on
shady stream banks in pine forests.

Variegated Comfrey   This striking variegated
perennial is a form of wild comfrey *Symphytum ×
uplandicum*. It needs deep, rich, moist soil and sun
or partial shade to be really impressive.

PLANTING HELP   Plant in damp, moderately
fertile soil in shade or partial shade. Can be easily
grown from seed, propagated by root division in
spring or by root cuttings at the beginning of the
winter. Comfrey makes an excellent compost and
when added to other plant materials will help
them to decompose quickly. Generally untroubled
by pests and diseases.

Variegated Comfrey

Lungwort

There are about 15 different *Pulmonarias* in the
wild. Mountain plants from S England to E
Europe, they make good garden plants and are
extremely valuable as ground-cover. All are
evergreen except *Pulmonaria angustifolia*. The
flowers, which appear in spring and last until early
summer, are followed by dense clumps of bold
leaves, variably hairy and often beautifully spotted
with silver. Medieval herbalists thought that
Pulmonaria was good for lung diseases – the leaf
spots looked like diseased lungs, hence the name.

PLANTING HELP   Suitable for moist places
between shrubs, the front of a border, wooded
gardens or grassy banks under trees. Grow in
moist, but not wet fertile soil with plenty of humus
in full or partial shade. Lungwort self-seeds freely
in gardens and to ensure a plant grows exactly like
its parent, the best form of propagation is division;

White Comfrey *Symphytum orientale*

it is also possible to grow plants from root cuttings. It is a good idea to divide and replant every four years or so. Slugs and snails are attracted to young leaves and mildew causes problems if the ground is too dry. Remove dead leaves after flowering

Pulmonaria angustifolia An herbaceous perennial spreading to form mats up to 10in (25cm) tall, producing clusters of bright blue flowers ½in (1cm) wide in spring. The unspotted leaves become larger after the flowers fade. Hardy to −20°F (−29°C), US zones 5–9. Native to much of western Europe and introduced into cultivation early in the 18th century.

Pulmonaria angustifolia

Soldiers and Sailors, Jerusalem Cowslip, Spotted Dog *Pulmonaria officinalis* Grows to 10in (25cm) tall and about 18in (45cm) wide, with reddish flowers that become blue in spring. Spotted heart-shaped leaves 6 × 4in (16 × 10cm). Hardy to −20°F (−29°C), US zones 5–9. Native across N Europe from west to east.

***Pulmonaria rubra* 'Redstart'** Often the first *Pulmonaria* to flower. Grows to 16in (40cm) tall and about 3ft (90cm) wide, producing orangy-red flowers from March to May, and bearing leaves 6 × 2½in (15 × 6cm), usually unspotted but hairy. Native to E Europe.

Soldiers and Sailors *Pulmonaria officinalis*

Soldiers and Sailors

Pulmonaria rubra 'Redstart'

Omphalodes

***Omphalodes cappadocica* 'Cherry Ingram'** Grows to 10in (25cm) tall, it will grow to form a clump about 12in (30cm) wide, with blue flowers in early spring. The leaves are narrower than the species, about 6½in (16.5cm) long.

PLANTING HELP Grow in a sheltered position in partial shade. Hardy to −10°F (−23°C), US zones 6–9.

Omphalodes 'Cherry Ingram'

Euphorbia amygdaloides 'Rubra'

Cardamine pentaphyllos

Euphorbia griffithii

Cardamine

Cardamine is a group of fleshy rooted perennials which thrive in cool shade. They are native to many parts of the Northern Hemisphere.

PLANTING HELP   For sandy leafy soil, kept moist in summer. Seeds should be planted in autumn or spring and plants can be divided after flowering before they die down. Slugs can be a problem.

Cardamine pentaphyllos (syns. *Dentaria digitata*, *D. pentaphyllos*)   A perennial which forms clumps of white or pale purple flowers in April. Stems 12–24in (30–60cm). Leaves made up of finger-like leaflets. Hardy to −10°F (−23°C), US zones 6–9. Native from the Pyrenees in Spain to C Europe, growing in woods and by streams in the mountains.

Cardamine heptaphylla (syn. *Dentaria pinnata*) This plant forms clumps of green leaves, produces clusters of white flowers, rarely pink or purplish. Stems 12–24in (30–60cm). Hardy to −10°F (−23°C), US zones 6–9. Native to SW and C Europe, growing in woods in the mountains.

Euphorbia

Spurge   Although the actual flowers of these plants are rather insignificant, the bracts which lie just beneath the petals are very attractive and have the added advantage of lasting for a long time.

PLANTING HELP   Beware! The sap from these plants can injure skin. For moist fertile soil

Woodspurge *Euphorbia amygdaloides* wild in Kent

in sun or partial shade. Plants can be divided in half in spring.

Woodspurge *Euphorbia amygdaloides* A bushy evergreen perennial producing subtle [illegible] [illegible] flowers from March to August. The stems are 2½ft (75cm) tall, leafy in the first year, flowering in the second. Hardy to 0°F (−18°C), US zones 7–10. Native to Europe and N Africa from Ireland to Algeria and eastwards to Poland, Turkey and the Caucasus, in woods, hedges and on grassy banks in rather moist soil. *E.* **'Rubra'** (syn. *Euphorbia amygdaloides* 'Purpurea') is a purple-leaved selection. Var. *robbiae* is a good suckering variety useful for ground-cover.

Euphorbia griffithii A spreading perennial that grows to 3ft (90cm) tall bearing orange flowers in early summer. The form 'Dixter' has lovely reddish-purple leaves. It grows best in damp semi-shade. Hardy to −20°F (−29°C), US zones 5–9.

Marsh Marigold

Marsh Marigold, Kingcup, Cowslip (in America) *Caltha palustris* At one time used in garlands for May Day festivals, this plant was thought to act as a cure for warts, anaemia and fits, but is, in fact, extremely poisonous. It is a perennial herb bearing attractive rounded leaves, ¼–¾in (5–20mm) long and produces stunning yellow flowers up to 2in (5cm) wide, in early spring. These plants require moist soil and do well on the edge of water. Hardy to 0°F (−18°C), US zones 7–10. Native to most of the N Hemisphere, in marshes, wet alder woods or by streams. *C. palustris* var. *alba* is an attractive white form.

PLANTING HELP Propagate by parting the roots in autumn and plant in moist soil or at the edge of a pond. Sometimes attacked by mildew.

Ourisia

New Zealand Mountain Foxglove *Ourisia macrophylla* An evergreen plant forming spreading mats of stems to 2ft (60cm) tall, producing white flowers ¾in (2cm) wide, in June. Hardy to −10°F (−23°C), US zones 6–9. Native to New Zealand, growing in damp shady places.

PLANTING HELP For peaty moist soil in partial shade and a cool position. Sow seed in early spring or take cuttings in early summer. Divide and replant every few years to maintain a healthy plant. May be attacked by slugs or snails.

Cardamine heptaphylla

Marsh Marigold *Caltha palustris*

Caltha palustris var. *alba*

Ourisia macrophylla

Epimediums at the PepsiCo Gardens, New York

Epimedium

Barrenwort, Bishop's Mitre   Deciduous or evergreen, epimediums make wonderful ground-cover, slowly increasing in sun or shade, but preferring cool shade. The foliage, particularly that of *E. × rubrum* and *E. × versicolor* is outstandingly attractive, displaying interesting colour in spring and autumn.

PLANTING HELP   Grow in fertile, moist, well-drained soil in partial shade. Foliage can be cut back in winter so that the flowers enjoy more prominence. Beware! flowers can be damaged by spring frosts. Propagate by division after flowering. Problems can arise from insects and slugs.

Epimedium grandiflorum (syn. *E. macranthum*)   A delicate deciduous plant forming small clumps 8–15in (20–38cm) wide, producing white, pink or purple flowers 1–1¾in (2.5–4.5cm) wide, from March to May. Hardy to –10°F (–23°C), US zones 6–9. Native to Japan, growing in moist woods in the hills. Several cultivars of this species are grown in Japan, Europe and North America.

Epimedium pinnatum   A tough, slow-growing evergreen plant forming dense clumps, bearing leaves 6in (15cm) long and producing flowers 1½in (4cm) wide, in April. Hardy to 0°F (–18°C), US zones 7–10. Native to NE Turkey eastwards to the W Caucasus mountains, growing in pine woods and azalea and oak scrub. *E. × perralchicum* 'Fröhnleiten' is the finest of this group.

***Epimedium × versicolor* 'Sulphureum'**   An evergreen plant forming a mound of leaves to 12in (30cm) tall and wide. Dark yellow flowers ¾in (2cm) wide, are produced from mid- to late spring. 'Sulphureum' has between 5 and 9 leaflets and a leafy flowering stem. Hardy to –10°F (–20°C), US zones 6–9. A hybrid between *Epimedium grandiflorum* and *Epimedium pinnatum* subsp. *colchicum*, known since 1854.

Epimedium × versicolor 'Sulphureum'

Epimedium × rubrum   A clump-forming evergreen perennial with stems to 8in (20cm) tall, producing flowers ¾–1in

Epimedium grandiflorum

Epimedium × rubrum

Epimedium pinnatum

Bleeding Heart *Dicentra spectabilis* at PepsiCo Gardens, New York

(2–2.5cm) wide, pale yellow with crimson inside. Very attractive red foliage when young and again when old; one of the most beautiful of all foliage plants for ground-cover. Hardy to 0°F (–18°C), US zones 7–10. A hybrid between *E. grandiflorum* and *E. alpinum* known since 1854.

Dicentra

A group of perennials growing in woodlands of Asia and North America, bearing many flowers on each stem; some are evenly spaced out along the stem, like *Dicentra spectabilis*, others are clustered at the end of the stems, like *Dicentra formosa* subsp. *oregona*. A very beautiful plant for a slightly shaded position, popular in cottage gardens. Contact with foliage can irritate skin.

Dicentra formosa subsp. *oregona* 'Langtrees'

PLANTING HELP   Plant in moist, possibly slightly acid fertile soil in partial shade. Divide or sow seed in spring or plant cuttings of *D. spectabilis* in winter. Slugs may be attracted to the plants.

Bleeding Heart *Dicentra spectabilis*   A clump-forming herbaceous perennial, 2ft (60cm) tall with arching stems, rather wider than tall. In late spring and early summer it produces locket-shaped rosy-pink and white flowers 1in (2.5cm) long, on stems held well above the fleshy brittle leaves. Hardy to

10°F (–12°C), US zones 8–10. Native to N China and introduced into cultivation early in the 19th century. There is also a fine white form, 'Alba', with greyish leaves.

***Dicentra formosa* subsp. *oregona* 'Langtrees'**
This plant forms small patches of stems 10in (25cm) long, bearing beautiful deeply divided leaves to 20in (50cm), but usually 10in (25cm) in length, above which the strangely shaped little flowers, with yellowish outer petals and pink-tipped inner ones, dangle in branching drooping sprays during April and May. Hardy to 0°F (–18°C), US zones 7–10. Native to Oregon, USA.

Dame's Violet

Dame's Violet *Hesperis matronalis*
A short-lived perennial which grows to 4ft (1.2m) tall, forming clumps of erect stems, producing open clusters of white, pink or purplish flowers about 1in (2.5cm) wide, in early summer. Strongly scented in the evening. The leaves are to 6in (15cm) long. Hardy to −20°F (−29°C), US zones 5–9. Native to S Europe. A delightful plant for a damp shady place where the evening scent can be enjoyed. Self-seeds freely, and in some areas, such as in eastern Scotland, has become a conspicuous feature of damp roadsides and streambanks. There are also some rare double-flowered varieties which are difficult to grow.

PLANTING HELP   Plant in autumn or early spring in any damp soil in a partially shaded position. It is free from pests and diseases.

Honesty

Honesty can be annual, biennial or perennial, and is often found growing wild in recently disturbed ground. The very attractive rounded seed pods are frequently dried and used in flower arrangements, particularly at Christmas.

PLANTING HELP   Plant *Lunaria annua* seeds in early summer and the perennial *Lunaria redidiva* in spring, in moist fertile soil in sun or partial shade. Propagate by division in spring.

Honesty, **Satin Flower** *Lunaria annua*
A biennial to 3ft (90cm) tall and 1ft (30cm) wide, producing unscented purple or white flowers 1in (2.5cm) across in late spring and summer. Hardy to −10°F (−23°C), US zones 6–9. Native to much of Europe.

Perennial Honesty *Lunaria redidiva*
A perennial bearing stems 14in–4½ft (35–140cm) long, which elongate during flowering in May. The pale pink or white flowers are deliciously scented, especially in the evening. Hardy to −10°F (−23°C), US zones 6–9. Native to most of Europe, east to Siberia in moist, usually subalpine woods and scrub in the mountains in the south, but not common.

Baneberry *Actaea rubra* f. *neglecta*

Perennial Honesty *Lunaria redidiva*

Dame's Violet *Hesperis matronalis*

Honesty *Lunaria annua*

Pachyphragma macrophyllum

Baneberry

Actaea rubra* f. *neglecta (syn. *A. erythrocarpa*)
This perennial grows to 1½ft (45cm) tall and
forms clumps with several stems, bearing leaves to
15in (38cm) long. Clusters of white flowers are
borne from mid-spring to early summer and white
berries succeed the flowers. Hardy to −10°F
(−23°C), US zones 6–9. Native to woods of North
America.

PLANTING HELP   For leafy soil in shade or
partial shade. Propagate by division in spring.

Pachyphragma

Pachyphragma macrophyllum   An almost-
evergreen perennial with flowering stems to 4in
(10cm) tall, producing scented white flowers in
April to May. Hardy to 0°F (−18°C), US zones
7–10. Native to NE Turkey and the W Caucasus,
usually growing in wet beech forests.

PLANTING HELP   For moist leafy soil in
damp shade. Sow seeds in autumn or divide in
spring. Slugs may cause problems.

Oxlip *Primula elatior*

Candelabra Primula *Primula prolifera*

Primula whitei 'Sherriff's Variety'

Primrose

When primroses begin to flower, spring cannot be very far away. There are several hundred different species belonging to this genus, ranging from those which prefer sun to those which tolerate deep shade. They vary considerably but can roughly be categorized into the evergreen auriculas, the taller candelabras which die right back in winter and the Primrose-Polyanthus group, evergreen or deciduous, including the wild primrose of Europe and Turkey. Most primroses prefer partial shade, although *Primula bhutanica* and some of the cultivars of primrose will thrive in more intense shade. Many other shade-loving species may be difficult to find in nurseries.

PLANTING HELP   Plant in rich, deep, moist, fertile soil in autumn or spring with protection from extreme wet in winter. Most species prefer slightly chalky soil with additional peat and leaf-mould for the Himalayan species. Many are short-lived and best raised from seed every four years or so. Most old-named primroses suffer from a virus which weakens them. Although they self-seed freely, and indeed can become invasive in some gardens, their seeds do not always produce a plant exactly like the parent, and propagation by division between autumn and early spring is a more reliable alternative. At the end of winter it is a good idea to trim off any old dead stems and leaves to preserve a tidy appearance. Greenfly on the undersides of the leaves or around the roots can kill the plants in dry weather.

Candelabra Primula *Primula prolifera* (syn. *P. helodoxa*)   An evergreen perennial that grows to 2½ft (75cm) tall and produces flowers, each about ¾in (2cm) wide, in summer. Hardy to −10°F (−23°C), US zones 6–9. Native to W China, Burma and the Himalayas, it is one of the candelabra primulas, so-called because of the tiered arrangement of its flowers.

Primula flaccida

Wild Primrose *Primula vulgaris*

Primula vulgaris subsp. *sibthorpii* from Greece

Oxlip *Primula elatior*   An evergreen or semi-evergreen perennial, easily grown in shade or partial shade, producing a spray of pale yellow flowers to 1in (2.5cm) long, on stems 4–12in (10–30cm) long. Leaves 4–8in (10–20cm) long. Hardy to –10°F (–23°C), US zones 6–9. Native to N Europe, growing in woods and meadows.

***Primula whitei* 'Sherriff's Variety'** (syn. *P. bhutanica)*   An easily grown deciduous plant which spreads rapidly, forming clusters of white buds that become stemless pin-eyed flowers ¾–1in (2–2.5cm) wide, from February to March. Leaves to 8in (20cm) long. This plant must be planted in total shade and the soil kept moist. Hardy to –30°F (–35°C), US zones 4–8. Native to a small area in NE India, growing in forests and under rhododendrons.

Primula flaccida (syn. *P. nutans)*   Easily grown in a partially shaded position, this deciduous plant is short-lived but can be raised from seed without difficulty. Stems to 20in (50cm) long, with dense heads of spicily scented flowers to 2in (5cm) long and to 1in (2.5cm) across. Leaves 8in (20cm) long. Hardy to 0°F (–18°C), US zones 7–10. Native to SE China, growing in pine forest and rocky pastures, dry in winter.

Primrose *Primula vulgaris*   An evergreen or semi-evergreen perennial that grows to 6in (15cm) tall, leaves to 4in (10cm) long, forming rosettes of fragrant pale yellow flowers with prominent deep-yellow eyes 1¼in (3cm) wide, in early spring. Hardy to –20°F (–29°C), US zones 5–9. Native to much of Europe, W Asia and N America, where it commonly grows wild in woods, hedgerows and pastures.

Primula vulgaris* subsp. *sibthorpii (syn. *Primula sibthorpii)*   Similar but with purplish-pink or red flowers from March to April. Hardy to 0°F (–18°C), US zones 7–10. Native to eastern Europe and western Asia.

Virginia Cowslip

Brunnera macrophylla

Brunnera macrophylla

Brunnera

Brunnera macrophylla A perennial forming clumps up to 1ft (30cm) tall and wider, producing sprays of intense blue flowers ½in (1.5cm) wide, in early spring. The broad heart-shaped leaves, sometimes splashed with silver, enlarge after flowering to 6in (15cm) or longer. Hardy to −10°F (−23°C), US zones 6–9. Native to the Caucasus, from where it was introduced into cultivation early in the 18th century. Plant in autumn or spring, in soil that is not too dry in a partially shaded position. It provides lovely ground-cover for a shady spot, with vivid flowers and handsome leaves.

***Brunnera macrophylla* 'Hadspen Cream'** Has boldly variegated leaves with a rather narrow creamy white margin.

PLANTING HELP Plant in autumn or spring, in any soil that is not too dry in a partially shaded position. Free from pests and diseases.

Mertensia

Virginia Cowslip, Blue Bells *Mertensia pulmonarioides* (syn. *M. virginica*) Said to capture the very essence of spring, this perennial grows to 24in (60cm) tall, bearing greyish leaves to 6in (15cm) long, which blend perfectly with clusters of nodding light blue flowers about 1in (2.5cm) long, in spring. Hardy to −30°F (−35°C), US zones 4–8. Native to E North America and introduced into cultivation in the 19th century.

PLANTING HELP Plant in autumn or late spring in moist peaty soil in sun or partial shade;

Brunnera macrophylla 'Hadspen Cream'

Forget-me-nots growing with wallflowers and tulips

ensure that young plants are shaded and soil kept moist. Divide in spring or take root cuttings when plant is dormant. Generally free from diseases, but may be plagued by slugs and snails.

Forget-me-not

Forget-me-not *Myosotis sylvatica*

Forget-me-not *Myosotis sylvatica*   A biennial or short-lived perennial that grows to 1ft (30cm) tall, forming a clump as wide as tall. In spring it produces the familiar sprays of small clear blue flowers about ½in (1.5cm) wide. The hairy oblong leaves are up to 4in (10cm) in length. Hardy to −20°F (−29°C), US zones 5–9. Native to most of Europe, N Africa and W Asia, and long

Forget-me-not

cultivated. *Myosotis sylvatica* has produced many garden varieties, including ugly dwarf forms as well as ones with white, dark blue or pink flowers. It is a much-loved cottage garden flower, easily grown and often sowing itself after the first year.

PLANTING HELP   Seeds of this biennial are normally sown in summer for flowering the following spring. It will grow in any soil in partial shade or in full sun if shaded at midday. It is generally free from pests but the leaves may become mildewed in hot dry conditions. Pull up the dying plants in midsummer and throw them onto bare ground. Hundreds of seedlings will appear in autumn.

Granny's Bonnet *Aquilegia vulgaris*

Aquilegia 'Hensol Harebell'

American Columbine *Aquilegia canadensis*

Viola odorata 'Alba'

Aquilegia

The Latin word *Aquilegia* and the common name Columbine refer to, respectively, eagle- or dove-shaped flowers of these herbaceous perennials; the petals resemble the extended wings, and the spur which contains the nectar and protrudes from the centre of the petals, the head and neck. Long cultivated in cottage gardens, these plants vary in colour when raised from seed and are an attractive addition to any garden.

PLANTING HELP   Plant in autumn or early spring in moist well-drained soil and in a cool position in deciduous shade. *Aquilegia canadensis* needs a sandy soil. These plants self-seed freely but will hybridize and therefore, to preserve the colour of the parent, it is best to plant them at a long distance from other aquilegia plants.

***Aquilegia* 'Hensol Harebell'**   An old hybrid strain between *A. alpina* and *A. vulgaris* which comes true from seed. Masses of large blue flowers in May. Stems to 3½ft (1m) tall. Easily grown and self-sows. Hardy to −10°F (−23°C), US zones 6–9.

Sweet White Violet *Viola blanda*

English Violet *Viola odorata*

American Columbine *Aquilegia canadensis*
Grows to 2ft (60cm) tall, producing flowers 1¼in
(3cm) wide in summer, which are pollinated by
hummingbirds. Hardy to −40°F (−40°C), US
zones 3–8 or lower. Native to E North America
growing in rocky woods and on shady banks and
damp roadsides. It needs direct sun for part of
the day. Introduced into cultivation in the 17th
century.

Granny's Bonnet *Aquilegia vulgaris*   Grows to
3ft (90cm) tall and bearing attractive grey foliage.
From May to July pale green stems and buds
produce nodding flowers 1½in (4cm) wide,
usually purplish-blue or pink, sometimes
reddish, purple or white. Hardy to
−30°F (−35°C), US zones 4–8 or
lower. Native to much of
Europe growing in woods
and meadows.

Violets

The many different
pansies and violets,
comprising annuals and
perennials, deciduous and
evergreen, are native to
various habitats in
temperate regions
throughout the
world. The origin of
the generic name is a
little uncertain but one
suggestion is that *viola* is
the Latin form of the
Greek *Ione*. Io, beloved
of Jupiter, was turned by
him into a heifer and violets
sprang up around her as
food!

Horned
Pansy

PLANTING HELP   Plant in autumn or spring
in fertile damp soil in sun or partial shade and
protect from wet in winter, although it is
important to keep plants moist in hot weather.
Annual replanting in spring can be beneficial,
removing old flower heads will lengthen flowering
time and plants can be cut back to maintain their
shape. Propagate by division or take cuttings in
spring or autumn. May be attractive to slugs and
snails, and can be affected by mildew.

Sweet White Violet *Viola blanda*   A stemless
plant to about 2in (5cm) tall with a slender
rootstock, thin leafy runners and dark purple seed
capsules. Slightly scented white flowers are
produced during April and May. For a cool shady
position. Hardy to −40°F (−40°C), US zones 3–8.
Native to North America flowering in mountains
and cool rocky woods.

Horned Pansy, Viola *Viola cornuta*   A perennial
that grows to 9in (23cm) tall producing a
succession of deep violet flowers, each about 1in
(2.5cm) wide, in summer. The leaves are 1in
(2.5cm) long and the fruit is an insignificant pod
with many small seeds. For sun or partial shade.
Hardy to −10°F (−23°C), US zones 6–9. Native to
the Pyrenees, this plant is an important parent of
many attractive and reliably perennial violas now
available. It is a good edging plant and is not out
of place on a shady rock garden.

Sweet Violet, English Violet, *Viola odorata*   A
sweet-scented semi-evergreen perennial with leaf
stalks to 5in (12cm) long and flower stems to 2in
(5cm) long, bearing deep purple or white flowers
½in (1.5cm) across, from February to May. Hardy
to −10°F (−23°C), US zones 6–9. Native to much
of Europe, *Viola odorata* has been used since
ancient times in perfume, confectionery, wine,
cosmetics and medicine. **'Alba'** has white flowers.

Umbrella Leaf *Diphylleia cymosa*

Diphylleia

Umbrella Leaf *Diphylleia cymosa*   A large
perennial forming a dense clump of stems to 3½ft
(1m) tall, bearing 2-lobed leaves 4–15in (10–38cm)
across. Umbels of flowers are produced from May
to June and the attractive dark blue berries, ½in
(1.5cm) long, are enhanced by the stalks which
turn red in autumn. Hardy to 0°F
(−18°C), US zones 7–10. Native to USA in the
Appalachians, growing by mountain streams.
Umbrella Leaf is so-called because of its immense
two-lobed rounded leaves.

PLANTING HELP   Plant in moist leafy soil in
shade or partial shade and shelter from cold
winds. Sow seed in containers when ripe and
divide in spring. Slugs and snails may be attracted
to the buds and young leaves.

Hacquetia

Hacquetia epipactis (syn. *Dondia epipactis*)
This plant produces delightful tiny yellow flowers
framed by green petal-like leaves called bracteoles,
from March to May. The stems, usually about 4in
(10cm) long, can reach 10in (25cm) when they
elongate during flowering. Native to the Alps,
eastwards to E Europe. Hardy to −10°F (−23°C),
US zones 6–9.

PLANTING HELP   Plant in a moist shady
position in humus-rich soil and propagate by
division after flowering. Beware of slugs and snails
in spring when young leaves appear.

Hacquetia epipactis

Jeffersonia

Jeffersonia dubia (syn. *Plagiorhegma dubia*)
A small perennial with stems to 8in (20cm) long,
bearing leaves 4in (10cm) across and producing
single lavender or occasionally white flowers 1in
(2.5cm) across, in April or May. Hardy to −10°F
(−23°C), US zones 6–9. Native to forest and scrub
in NE Asia.

PLANTING HELP   Plant in moist peaty soil in
partial or full shade. Sow seed in containers when
ripe. Divide plants in spring. Slugs may be
attracted to young leaves.

Wood Sorrel

Oxalis acetosella   A pretty, spreading clover-
like plant with leaf stalks 2–6in (5–15cm) tall, and
flowers ½in (1.5cm) wide, usually white with lilac
veins, rarely pinkish. Hardy to −20°F (−29°C),
US zones 5–9. Native to Europe and North

Jeffersonia dubia

America, growing in moist woods, moorlands and on shady rocks

PLANTING HELP Needs moist leafy soil and shade in summer. Can be divided in spring.

Podophyllum

Podophyllum hexandrum (syn. *Podophyllum emodi*) A perennial forming a clump of stems to 1ft (30cm) long at flowering time, taller later. Apple-like cup-shaped flowers with petals to 1.5in (4cm) are produced in May and June, followed by shiny red fruit. The attractive pairs of 3-lobed leaves, variably marked with purple, unfurl after flowering, finally reaching 5–14in (12–35cm) across. Native to India, Afghanistan and China, growing in scrub, forest and alpine meadows. Although it is used medicinally in India, it is much stronger than the American species *Podophyllum peltatum* and should not be used as a herbal substitute. Extracts of *Podophyllum* species are being studied as a possible cancer treatment, but most species are too toxic for internal use.

PLANTING HELP Grow in moist fertile soil in sun or partial shade. Sow seed in containers when ripe. Divide in spring or early autumn. Slugs are attracted to young leaves.

Wood sorrel *Oxalis acetosella*

Podophyllum hexandrum

Uvularia

Large Merrybells *Uvularia grandiflora*
A dainty woodland perennial with stems to 2½ft (75cm) long, bearing leaves 2–5in (5–12cm) long, producing bell-like, bright yellow flowers 1–2in (2.5–5cm) wide, either singular or in pairs, in April or May. Hardy to −10°F (−23°C), US zones 6–9. Native to woods of North America.

PLANTING HELP Easily grown in moist leafy soil in deciduous shade. Sow seed in containers when ripe. Divide in spring. Needs protection from slugs when young.

Large Merrybells

Large Merrybells *Uvularia grandiflora*

Dog's Tooth Violet *Erythronium dens-canis*

Yellow Adder's Tongue *Erythronium americanum*

Erythronium 'Pagoda'

Bluebell

Wild Hyacinth
Hyacinthoides non-scripta
(syn. *Endymion non-scriptus*)
The common bluebell
grows 8–20in (20–50cm)
tall and produces
one-sided
drooping stems of
fragrant tubular
flowers, usually blue
but occasionally
white or pink, in
spring. Hardy to
−10°F (−23°C),
US zones 6–9.
Native to W Europe
where it often grows in its
millions in woods or shady
meadows.

PLANTING HELP
Plant 3in (8cm) deep in
reasonably moist well-
drained soil in partial shade
in autumn. Bluebells are
prolific seeders, but pulling
up flowers as they fade will
prevent them from spreading
too widely.

Bluebells

Erythronium

There are about 20 different types of *Erythronium*
from diverse native habitats in Europe, Asia and
North America. The variety of their flowers and
foliage provides an interesting addition to the
spring and summer garden.

PLANTING HELP   Bulbs should be planted
in autumn in partial shade to a depth of 4in
(10cm) in moist, fertile soil rich in humus. It is
important to keep them slightly damp during
storage if they are not planted immediately after
purchase. Once they are wellestablished, the
clumps of plants can be divided when dormant.
Slugs may be a problem.

Dog's Tooth Violet *Erythronium dens-canis*
The variably-spotted leaves are 4–6in (10–15cm)
long when fully grown and are particularly well
marked in some forms from Italy. White, lilac or
pink flowers to 1¼–1½in (3–4cm) across with
purple or blue centres, are produced in spring.
Hardy to 0°F (−18°C), US zones 7–10. Native
across S Europe. Easy to grow in leafy soil or thin
grass in half-shade.

Wild Bluebells under Silver Birch trees in a Kentish woodland

Yellow Adder's Tongue, Trout Lily, Amberbell
Erythronium americanum A small bulb that grows to 6in (15cm) tall. Flowering from late March to June, it is distinguished by its small size, mottled leaves and yellow flowers which only open in the warm sun. The flowers are brownish orange. Grows well in moist sandy soil under deciduous trees. Hardy to −30°F (−35°C), US zones 4–8. Native to E North America.

Erythronium **'Pagoda'** This plant bears bronze-mottled green leaves and pale yellow flowers on stems 6–14in (15–35cm) tall. Hardy to 0°F (−18°C), US zones 7–10. A hybrid between *E. tuolumnense* and one of the white-flowered species. Very vigorous and easily grown in rich leafy soil under the shade of deciduous trees.

Nectaroscordum

Nectaroscordum siculum A fascinating bulb bearing grassy and very smelly leaves 12–16in (30–40cm) long, and producing heads of drooping bell-like flowers ½–1in (1.5–2.5cm) across, in May. Hardy to 0°F (−18°C), US zones 7–10. A relative of garlic, native of S Europe from France

eastwards to Bulgaria and the Crimea and Turkey, growing in damp shady woods. The plants from Italy westwards have dull greenish-red flowers whereas those in Turkey and Bulgaria eastwards have whitish flowers shaded with green and pink.

PLANTING HELP
Plant in light soil in sun or partial shade. Sow seed in containers in autumn or spring. Makes an interesting addition to any border.

Nectaroscordum siculum

Ramsons *Allium ursinum*

Trillium grandiflorum

Arum italicum subsp. *italicum* 'Marmoratum'

Allium

There are around 700 different types of onion which are bulbs or perennials, mainly from the Northern Hemisphere, that flower in spring, summer and autumn. Several, including garlic, chives and onions, have culinary uses. Most of these decorative garden plants need full sun but the following are woodland plants and will thrive in partial shade.

PLANTING HELP   Plant bulbs approximately 3in (8cm) deep in autumn, and place rhizomes just below the surface in spring. Sow seed or divide in spring. Contact with bulbs may irritate skin. Can suffer from mildew.

Three-cornered Leek *Allium triquetrum*
Three-cornered leek can be distinguished easily from most other species by its triangular stem and distinctive flowers. The rather soft flat leaves appear in autumn and the nodding bluebell-shaped flowers in April. Hardy to 10°F (–12°C), US zones 8–10. Growing in warm places in hedges and by roadsides where it has escaped from cottage gardens. Native to W Mediterranean region, found naturalized in hedgebanks and waste places in other parts of Europe, growing in damp shady places often by streams.

Ramsons, Bear's Garlic or **Wood Garlic** *Allium ursinum*
A perennial herb with a white bulb from which the flowering stems grow to 4–18in (10–45cm) tall. The six-petalled sweetly scented white flowers grow in a cluster at the top of the stem and bloom in April, May or June. The small black seeds are contained in a three-chambered capsule and are dispersed by black ants. Native to Europe and Asia Minor, often found growing in damp woods, shady places and along stream banks. Hardy to –20°F (–29°C), US zone 5–9. A relative of cultivated garlic, the fresh young leaves can be gathered in spring and used in salads, the freshly pressed juice is commonly used in slimming diets and can also be made into a syrup to soothe coughs and colds.

Three-cornered Leek
Allium triquetrum

Zantedeschia aethiopica in Italy

Arisaema sikokianum

Arisaema

Arisaema sikokianum A bulb bearing handsome leaves and producing flowers, each about 3–5in (8–12cm) tall, in spring before the leaves have fully developed. The flowers are of variable colouring but usually the half-petal, called a spathe, is chocolate-brown outside and green-striped inside, and surrounds a white knob, called a spadix. Insignificant flowers are borne at the base of the spadix followed by spikes of colourful berries. Hardy to 0°F (−18°C), US zones 7–10, but dislikes late frosts. Native to woods in Japan.

PLANTING HELP   Plant 4in (10cm) deep in moist fertile soil in shade or partial shade. Sow seed in containers in autumn or spring. Remove and replant offshoots in late summer. Is attractive to slugs and damaged by late frosts.

Arum

Arum italicum* subsp. *italicum **'Marmoratum'** (syn. *A. italicum* 'Pictum') A plant that grows to 2ft (60cm) tall producing pale creamy yellow flowers, each with a hooded half-petal called a spathe, about 6in (15cm) tall, in spring. Attractive but poisonous red fruiting heads are produced in late summer and beautiful pale green or cream-veined leaves appear in autumn. Hardy to 0°F (−18°C), US zones 7–10. Native to south and west Europe and N Africa in hedges and rocky places, often among old walls.

PLANTING HELP   Plant 4–6in (10–15cm) deep in spring or autumn in fertile well-drained soil in sun or partial shade. Sow seed in containers in autumn or divide after flowering.

Trillium

Wake Robin, Wood Lily, Birthroot *Trillium grandiflorum* A deciduous perennial that grows to 18in (45cm) tall with flowers 2–3in (5–8cm) wide that open white in spring and later become flushed with rose pink. There are also forms with double or deep pink flowers. Hardy to −20°F (−29°C), US zones 5–9, thriving in areas with wet summers. Native to E North America where it carpets the woods like Bluebells do in England.

PLANTING HELP   Plant 2in (5cm) deep in moist cool woodland conditions in good soil. Sow seed in containers when ripe or divide plants after flowering. Young leaves are attractive to slugs.

Zantedeschia

Zantedeschia aethiopica An herbaceous perennial up to 4ft (1.2m) tall producing spectacular white flowers from May onwards. Each flower is folded into a funnel shape up to 10in (25cm) long, surrounding a light yellow cone. The leaves are arrow-shaped, rich green and about 1ft (30cm) long. Hardy to −10°F (−23°C), US zones 6–9. Native to South Africa. This is a colourful plant for a bog garden or pool side.

PLANTING HELP   Plant in autumn or spring in moist or wet soil in sun or partial shade. Sow seed indoors when ripe, divide plant in spring. Sap may irritate skin. May be affected by aphids.

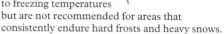

Camellia sasanqua 'Mine-no-yuki'

Camellias

The magnificent flowers of the camellia, simple or complex, solitary or paired, lend an exotic touch to the spring garden, and the rich evergreen foliage should not be ignored for its elegant simplicity. Camellias will tolerate occasional drops to freezing temperatures but are not recommended for areas that consistently endure hard frosts and heavy snows.

Camellia sasanqua 'Narumigata'

PLANTING HELP   Happiest in areas of light shade under mature trees, camellias benefit when sheltered from cold winds and the early morning sun; buds and flowers may be damaged by icy winds and late frosts. Plant in autumn or late spring in a well-drained acid or neutral soil using plenty of humus. Unless training into a two-dimensional shape, be careful not to place large plants too close to a wall as they can become lopsided. Little pruning is needed, although young plants can be lightly trimmed to encourage them to bush out. Scale insects may be a problem, resulting in an unsightly sooty mould on the leaves, but camellias are not generally affected by pests or diseases. Propagate by means of semi-ripe cuttings in autumn or leaf-bud cuttings in spring. Water well regularly but infrequently; more when in flower and in summer, sparingly in winter.

Camellia sasanqua   Flowering from October to December, this upright shrub to 13ft (4m) tall produces scented white flowers 1½–3in (4–8cm) across and dark glossy green leaves 1½–3½in (4–9cm) long. Native to Japan where the leaves were used to make a rather inferior tea, and, oil from the seeds is used for lighting, lubrication, cooking and cosmetics; even today the seeds are used in a variety of cottage industries. There are numerous cultivars, mostly with single or double pink or red flowers.

Camellia × williamsii 'E. G. Waterhouse'

Camellia sasanqua 'Hugh Evans'

Camellia sasanqua 'Hugh Evans'
(syn. 'Hebe') A strong-growing shrub with single, medium-sized pink flowers produced in autumn. The weeping branches enable it to be easily trained on a post or fence. Hardy to 10°F (−12°C), US zones 8–10.

Camellia sasanqua 'Mine-no-yuki'
(syn. 'White Dove') A bushy pendulous shrub, producing small to semi-double fragrant creamy flowers, useful for framing gateways or doors from mid-autumn to early winter. Hardy to 10°F (−12°C), US zones 8–10.

Camellia sasanqua 'Narumigata' Grows to 15ft (4.5m) tall, producing single white fragrant flowers about 2½–3in (6–8cm) wide, becoming slightly tinged with pink as they age in late autumn and early winter. Hardy to 10°F (−12°C), US zones 8–10.

Camellia × williamsii A group of hybrid Camellias first produced in the early 1930s by J. C. Williams of Caerhays Castle, Cornwall, England; the result of crossing *Camellia japonica* with *Camellia saluenensis*. Broadly oval, glossy green leaves with a fine point, up to 4in (10cm) long and flowers that drop as they die, ensuring a tidy plant.

Camellia × williamsii 'Anticipation' Grows to 15ft (4.5m) tall, erect but bushy in habit, producing abundant double rose pink flowers 4in (10cm) wide, in spring. Raised in New Zealand in 1962. Hardy to 10°F (−12°C), US zones 8–10.

Camellia × williamsii 'Bow Bells' Grows to 12ft (3.5m) tall, this compact bushy camellia is particularly suitable for growing up a shady wall. Often flowering exceptionally early, bearing large numbers of medium, trumpet-shaped, single pink flowers from mid-winter to late-spring. Hardy to 10°F (−12°C), US zones 8–10.

Camellia × williamsii 'E. G. Waterhouse'
A compact upright medium-sized plant of which there is also a variegated form, producing double light pink flowers in mid-spring. A self-grown seedling from the garden of Prof. E. G. Waterhouse of New South Wales, Australia. Hardy to 10°F (−12°C), US zones 8–10.

Camellia × williamsii 'Jury's Yellow'
An erect compact plant to 12ft (3.5m) tall, producing semi-double white flowers, with smaller yellow central petals. This cultivar was raised in New Zealand in 1976. Hardy to 10°F (−12°C), US zones 8–10.

Camellia × williamsii 'Jury's Yellow'

Camellia × williamsii 'Anticipation'

Camellia × williamsii 'Bow Bells'

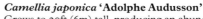

Camellia japonica 'Adolphe Audusson'
Grows to 20ft (6m) tall, producing an abundance
of semi-double, deep red flowers about 4in (10cm)
wide, with a few yellow stamens in the centre.
Raised in France in the late 19th century. Hardy to
10°F (−12°C), US zones 8–10.

Camellia 'Adolphe Audusson Variegated'
Flowers with occasional white
blotching. A variegated
sport of 'Adolphe
Audusson'.

Camellia japonica
'Lavinia Maggi'

Camellia japonica
'Jupiter' (syns. 'Juno',
'Sylvia') An upright
vigorous shrub to
15ft (4.5m)
producing single red
flowers with overlapped petals in
spring. Introduced into cultivation in
about 1900 by William Paul of
Cheshunt. Hardy to 10°F (−12°C),
US zones 8–10.

*Camellia
japonica*
'Jupiter'

Camellia japonica Forms of this species are
amoung the most common found in cultivation.
This large much-branched shrub or small tree
bears beautiful glossy leaves to 4in (10cm) long. It
is best trimmed into a more compact shape to
encourage flowering and to maintain a tidy
appearance. Native to Japan and introduced into
cultivation in the 18th century.

Camellia japonica
'Lady Clare' (syn. 'Akashigata') A pendulous
shrub to 15ft (4.5m) tall, producing semi-double,
deep rose pink flowers with yellow stamens, about

Camellia japonica 'Lady Clare' in Eccleston
Square

Camellia 'Cornish Snow'

4½in (11cm) wide, from early to late spring. It was introduced from Japan in the late 19th century. Hardy to 10°F (−12°C), US zones 8–10.

Camellia japonica 'Lavinia Maggi'
(syn. 'Contessa Lavinia Maggi') An erect shrub that grows to 15ft (4.5m) tall, bearing striking double white flowers splashed and striped with carmine red, 3½in (9cm) wide, in spring. Raised in Italy in the middle of the 19th century. Hardy to 10°F (−12°C), US zones 8–10.

Camellia japonica 'Mathotiana Rosea'
Grows to 15ft (4.5m) tall with a profusion of double flowers 4in (10cm) wide, with overlapping deep rosy pink petals in spring. A sport of 'Mathotiana Alba' that arose in the late 19th century. Hardy to 10°F (−12°C), US zones 8–10.

Camellia japonica 'Tricolor' An erect plant that grows to 20ft (6m) tall producing semi-double white or pale pink flowers marked with red, 4in (10cm) wide, in spring. Introduced from Japan around 1830. Hardy to 10°F (−12°C), US zones 8–10.

Camellia 'Cornish Snow' A first-rate shrub for planting against a wall; even with easterly exposure, this plant will reach to 15ft (4.5m) tall, producing single white flowers about 1½in (4cm) wide, with outer petals often flushed light pink. The glossy deep green leaves are narrowly oval with a fine point, 1½–3in (4–8cm) long. A hybrid betwen *C. cuspidata* and *C. saluenensis* raised by J. C. Williams in Cornwall, England in 1930. Hardy to 10°F (−12°C), US zones 8–10.

Camellia japonica 'Tricolor'

Camellia japonica 'Jupiter'

Camellia japonica 'Adolphe Audusson'

C. japonica 'Mathotiana Rosea'

Corylopsis sinensis var. *sinensis* in Brooklyn Botanic Garden, New York

Pieris 'Forest Flame'

Corylopsis

These deciduous shrubs and small trees, native to China, Japan and the E Himalayas, produce drooping clusters of of bell-shaped yellow flowers before the leaves appear in spring.

PLANTING HELP   Plant in moist acid soil in partial shade; if pruning is required, it should be carried out as soon as the plant has finished flowering. Propagate either by sowing seeds in autumn or by planting cuttings in summer. Free from pests and diseases, but damaged by late spring frosts.

Corylopsis sinensis* var. *sinensis
A deciduous shrub to 13ft (4m) tall, flowering in April. Flowers sweetly scented. Hardy to 0°F (−18°C), US zones 7 10. Native to China, growing in scrub and forest at 4550–7000ft (1300–2000m). ***Corylopsis sinensis* 'Veitchiana'** is a form or clone with bell-shaped flowers with red stamens. **'Spring Purple'** has attractive purplish young leaves.

Corylopsis sinensis 'Veitchiana'

Corylopsis sinensis 'Spring Purple'

Pieris 'Forest Flame' in Eccleston Square

Pieris

Evergreen shrubs which thrive in similar conditions to rhododendrons. Pieris are particularly renowned for the forms that produce bright red foliage in spring. They are well worth growing for their flowers alone, but these are eclipsed by the young foliage which gives a unique effect in open woodland.

PLANTING HELP   Plant in autumn or spring in acid or neutral soil in a slightly shaded position. Beware of late-spring frosts on new leaves. Pruning is not required but remove dead flowers to improve flowering next year. Propagate by taking cuttings in late summer. Free from pests and diseases, although leaf spot can sometimes be a problem.

Pieris **'Forest Flame'**   A vigorous evergreen shrub to 8ft (2.5m) tall producing drooping clusters, 4in (10cm) long, crowded with small bell-shaped white flowers, each ⅓in (1cm) long, in early spring. The leathery leaves are 3–5in (8–12cm) long and the shoots are bright scarlet in early spring, gradually changing through creamy-pink to the dark green of summer. Hardy to 0°F

(−18°C), US zones 7–10. A hybrid between the Japanese and Chinese species of pieris that arose as a chance seedling in Britain in the 20th century.

Chinese Pieris *Pieris formosa* var. *forrestii*   To 8ft (2.5m) tall, producing large creamy flowers during April and May which, contrasted with the young red foliage, creates a sensational spectacle. Hardy to 0°F (−18°C), US zones 7–10. Native of SW China, growing in Rhododendron scrub at 6500–9750ft (2000–3000m). The largest-flowered of the *Pieris* species, growing especially well on the East Coast of North America.

Chinese Pieris
Pieris formosa var. *forrestii*

Aucuba japonica
'Variegata'

Aucuba

Aucuba japonica 'Variegata' An evergreen shrub that grows to 10ft (3m) tall with spotted leaves bearing flowers of little garden value from March to May. Male and female flowers are on different plants, so both are required for the female to bear a good set of the attractive red berries. A very useful shrub for growing in shade. It was a popular plant in the late 19th century, often seen in Victorian shrubberies. Hardy to 0°F (−18°C), US zones 7–10. Native to Japan.

PLANTING HELP Very shade- and drought-tolerant. For any well-drained soil. Sow seed in containers or take root cuttings in summer.

Box

Boxwood *Buxus sempervirens*
A medium-sized evergreen shrub of dense bushy habit that grows to 16ft (4.5m) and about the same width. Very effective as a specimen, this form of Common Box is very amenable to judicious pruning. Hardy to 0°F (−18°C), US zones 7–10. Native to Europe, N Africa and Turkey.
Buxus sempervirens 'Aureovariegata' Almost circular leaves splashed, striped or mottled with creamy yellow.

Buxus sempervirens
'Aureovariegata'

Buxus sempervirens 'Latifolia Maculata' A slower-growing variety than most, with very dark green leaves marked with yellow patches.

PLANTING HELP Plant in any soil in sun or shade, although these plants appreciate good soil. Root semi-ripe cuttings in summer or graft in winter.

Buxus sempervirens
'Latifolia Maculata'

Euonymus

Euonymus japonicus A large dense evergreen shrub to 16ft (4.5m) tall, suitable for hedging as it stands clipping well. In early summer it produces clusters of small pale green flowers about ⅓in (1cm) wide. The glossy leaves are broadly oval or rounded and 1–3in (2.5–8cm) long. The fruit is a small reddish capsule which splits to show the orange seed. This shrub is highly valued in coastal gardens where its tolerance of salty winds makes it invaluable for hedging and shelter belts. Elsewhere its handsome foliage is a useful contrast to showier flowering plants. Hardy to 10°F (−12°C), US zones 8–10. Native to Japan and China.

PLANTING HELP Plant in autumn or early spring in any soil, in sun or shade; in cooler areas it will benefit from a sheltered site. No regular pruning is required other than cutting away the old damaged shoots.

Euonymus japonicus

Photinia

Photinia × fraseri 'Robusta' This shrub grows to 20ft (6m) tall and usually as wide. In late spring it produces broad clusters of flowers, each about ½in (1.5cm) wide. Hardy to 0°F (−18°C), US zones 7–10. *Photinia × fraseri* is a hybrid first raised in the USA, but 'Robusta' originated in Australia in this century. Valued for its brightly coloured young foliage, conspicuous well into the summer, this shrub is hardier than the similarly coloured Pieris and, unlike it, grows well in limy soils.

Photinia × fraseri 'Robusta'

Aucuba japonica 'Variegata'

PLANTING HELP Plant in fertile, moist, well-drained soil in sun or partial shade. Sow seed in containers in autumn, root cuttings indoors in summer. Can be affected by leaf spot.

Skimmia

A group of evergreen shrubs and trees from Asia which will tolerate shade, neglect and even pollution. Valuable for its flowers, some strongly scented, its foliage and fruit; both male and female plants are necessary to obtain fruit. Beware! the berries can cause stomach upset if eaten.

PLANTING HELP Plant in moist, fertile, well-drained soil in partial or full shade. Sow seed in autumn or root cuttings indoors in early autumn. May attract insects.

Skimmia japonica An evergreen shrub that grows to 7ft (2m) tall, but often more compact and usually rather wider than tall. In spring it bears compact conical clusters of small fragrant creamy white flowers, each about ⅓in (1cm) wide. Individual bushes have either male or female flowers, the males being particularly strongly scented. The leathery leaves are 2–3in (5–8cm)

long and have a curious oily scent when bruised. Where male and female bushes are grown together, the latter produce bright scarlet berries about ⅓in (1cm) wide. Hardy to 0°F (–18°C), US zones 7–10. Native to Japan.

***Skimmia japonica* 'Rubella'** A male clone, very attractive in bud, with particularly strongly scented flowers. As a male, it does not fruit, but is a good pollinator for any female variety planted with it.

Skimmia japonica 'Rubella'

Skimmia japonica

Magnolia soulangeana 'Rustica Rubra'at the Royal Botanic Gardens, Kew

Magnolias

Magnolias are believed to be among the most ancient of flowering plants, with fossil remains found in rocks over 2 million years old. One group originates from Central and North America and the other from Asia. Easily cultivated, deciduous or evergreen, varying from small shrubs to large trees, and producing flowers that differ in size, scent and colour. Magnolias can be seen in flower from February onward, for three-quarters of the year.

PLANTING HELP
Suitable for positions in sun or partial shade, most magnolias should be planted in deep, fertile acid or neutral soil, although a few, *M. wilsonii*, *M. × loebneri* 'Leonard Messel' will grow well

Magnolia sieboldii subsp. *sinensis*

Magnolia × loebneri 'Leonard Messel'

Wilson's Magnolia *Magnolia wilsonii*

Magnolia soulangeana 'Rustica Rubra'

'Rustica Rubra'

Grows to 25ft (8m) tall and wider, producing an abundance of slightly scented rosy red flowers, 5in (12cm) wide, before the leaves appear in spring; the petals are paler on the inside than the outside. The leaves are 3–6in (8–15cm) long and the fruit, curiously irregular in shape, is 3in (8cm) long, although it is not prolific. Hardy to –10°F (–23°C), US zones 6–9. A chance seedling from a Dutch nursery at the end of the 19th century.

Star Magnolia *Magnolia stellata* Grows to 10ft (3m) tall and wider, producing an abundance of sweetly scented flowers, 3–4in (8–10cm) wide, before the leaves appear in spring. The leaves are 2–4in (5–10cm) long and the seldom-produced cone-like fruit is 2in (5cm) long. Hardy to –20°F (–29°C), US zones 5–9. Native to Japan but now rare in the wild, introduced into cultivation in the late 19th century.

Wilson's Magnolia *Magnolia wilsonii* Arching branches to 25ft (8m) tall and wide, producing strongly scented, nodding, crimson-centred white flowers, 3–4in (8–10cm) across, before the leaves appear in spring. The leaves are 3–6in (8–15cm) long and the purplish-pink cone-like fruit about 3in (8cm) long. Hardy to 0°F (–18°C), US zones 7–10. Native to W China.

in any soil, even chalk. The roots of all magnolias are sensitive to disturbance. No regular pruning is needed, other than light shaping when young. They are not normally affected by pests and diseases, although young magnolias are vulnerable to attack from slugs during the first year of life and these must be controlled to prevent defoliation.

Magnolia × loebneri 'Leonard Messel'

A deciduous shrub that grows to 25ft (8m) tall, producing an abundance of slightly scented, starry lilac pink flowers, 4in (10cm) wide, in spring. The leaves are 3–5in (8–12cm) long and the rarely produced fruit is about 3in (8cm) long. Will grow well in any soil, even chalk. Raised at Nymans, Sussex, England at the beginning of the 20th century.

Magnolia sieboldii subsp. sinensis

A deciduous shrub that grows to 20ft (6m) tall and as wide, producing scented red-centred white flowers, 5in (12cm) wide, in late May and early June, with a second flowering in August. Leaves to 7 × 5in (18 × 12cm). The bark is an unusual fawn colour and the fruit is a cone, 3in (8cm) long, pale pink becoming brown with age. Hardy to –10°F (–23°C), US zones 6–9. Native to China.

Star Magnolia *Magnolia stellata*

Rhododendron & Azalea

Rhododendron
'Cilpinense'

The stunning flowers and handsome glossy green foliage of the rhododendron can transform a shady area. Evergreen and deciduous, ranging from plants of only a few inches to trees over 12ft (3.5m) tall, these woodland plants explode into a sea of colour in spring and early summer. Clusters of showy funnel- or bell-shaped flowers are produced in almost every colour, and many, particularly the deciduous azaleas, provide great scent and spectacular autumn colour. Rhododendrons are native to Asia, S Europe and to North America where the common rosebay is a feature of mountain woods in the Appalachians.

PLANTING HELP   Plant in autumn or spring in acid or neutral, lime-free soil, moist but not waterlogged, in a partially shaded, sheltered position; any good soil can be made suitable if enriched with well dug in leaf mould, bracken, well-rotted manure or peat. Early preparation of the ground prior to planting by adding 1–2oz per square yard (35–70gms per square metre) of sulphate of ammonia, can make all the difference between success and failure. Rhododendrons are little affected by pests or diseases, although leaf spot, blotches and mildew can be a problem. Layering is the most successful method of propagation, but evergreen Azaleas are easy to increase from cuttings, and collecting and growing the seed from deciduous azaleas is a simple, though rather slow, alternative. No pruning is necessary but removal of dead flower heads, if practical, encourages the development of new flower buds.

Rhododendron fulvum   This evergreen shrub has large, very glossy green leaves with brown red, fine, felt-like hairs beneath, and produces compact trusses of pink bell-shaped flowers, 1–1¾in (2.5–4.5cm) long, from May to June. Leaves 3–9in (8–23cm) long. Hardy to 0°F (–18°C), US zones 7–10. Native to China and Burma.

Rhododendron lutescens   An evergreen or partly deciduous shrub to 20ft (6m) tall, bearing leaves that are reddish when young. Heat- and drought-tolerant, this plant produces creamy yellow flowers during April and May. Hardy to 10°F (–12°C), US zones 8–10. Native to China. Tolerant of some lime in the soil.

Rhododendron yakushimanum   A hardy species, ideal for small gardens, this compact, slow-growing evergreen shrub, to 8ft (2.5m) tall, forms a dome-shaped bush. In early summer a profusion of bright pink buds open to white flowers 2in (5cm) wide. The leaves are oblong, about 4in (10cm) long. Hardy to –10°F (–23°C), US zones 6–9. Native to the Japanese island of Yakushima and introduced into cultivation in the 20th century. It is the parent of many dwarf hybrids.

Rhododendron 'Cilpinense'   A compact evergreen shrub to 3ft (90cm) tall with glossy dark leaves about 1½in (4cm) long. In early spring rose pink buds open into pure white flowers, 2½in (6cm) wide, flushed with pink on the outside; they are quickly damaged by frost, so are best kept in a sheltered position. Hardy to 10°F (–12°C), US zones 8–10. Raised in England in the 20th century.

Rhododendron 'Temple Belle'

***Rhododendron* 'Elizabeth'**   This evergreen shrub grows to 7ft (2m) tall and 10ft (3m) or more wide and produces trusses of bright red, funnel-shaped flowers 2¾in (7cm) across, in spring in such abundance that they can hide the foliage. Hardy to 0°F (−18°C), US zones 7–10. Raised by F. C. Puddle at Bodnant in Wales in 1933.

***Rhododendron* 'Purple Splendour'**
An evergreen shrub that grows to 7ft (2m) tall, bearing leaves 6in (15cm) long and producing trusses of up to 15 purple flowers 2¾in (7cm) across in early summer. Hardy to −10°F (−23°C), US zones 6–9. Raised by A. Waterer in England before 1900.

***Rhododendron* 'Temple Belle'**   A compact free-flowering evergreen shrub suitable for small gardens. Grows to 5ft (1.5m) tall and usually wider, producing drooping clusters of bell-shaped pink flowers 3in (8cm) wide, in late spring. Hardy to 0°F (−18°C), US zones 7–10. A hybrid raised at the Royal Botanic Gardens, Kew, England in the 20th century.

Rhododendron lutescens

Rhododendron fulvum

Rhododendron yakushinanum

Rhododendron 'Elizabeth'

Rhododendron 'Purple Splendor'

51

Evergreen Azaleas at Sandling Park

Rhododendron ***Vuyk's Scarlet***

Rhododendron dauricum **'Midwinter'** This deciduous shrub grows to 5ft (1.5m) tall and wide and produces trusses of widely tubular, rosy purple flowers to 2in (5cm) across, from mid- to late winter. The glossy leaves ½–1½in (1.5–4cm) long and scaly underneath, turn purplish brown in winter. Hardy to −20°F (−29°C), US zones 5–9. Native of Asia and in cultivation since 1780.

Rhododendron **'Narcissiflora'** An upright deciduous azalea that grows to 8ft (2.5m) tall, bearing scented double yellow flowers in late spring and early summer. In autumn the leaves become a beautiful bronze colour. Hardy to −20°F (−29°C), US zones 5–9. Raised by L. van Houtt in Belgium before 1871.

Rhododendron 'Narcissiflora'

Rhododendron dauricum 'Midwinter'

Rhododendron 'Blue Danube'

Rhododendron 'Blue Danube' ('Blaue Donau')   An evergreen azalea that grows to 7ft (2m) tall and wider, producing deep violet flowers from May to June. Hardy to −10°F (−23°C), US zones 6–9. A hybrid of uncertain partentage raised by A. Vuyk in Holland in 1921.

Rhododendron 'Hershey's Red'
A low-growing spreading evergreen azalea that grows to 7ft (2m) tall and wider, bearing small dark green ovate leaves and brightly coloured red flowers. Hardy to −10°F (−23°C), US zones 6–9. A hybrid raised by Ralph Hershey in Gap, Pennsylvania.

Rhododendron 'Hershey's Red'

Rhododendron 'Vuyk's Scarlet'
A compact evergreen azalea of spreading habit that grows to 3ft (90cm) tall, producing funnel-shaped crimson flowers 2in (5cm) wide, in late spring. Leaves oval 1in (2.5cm) long. Hardy to 0°F (−18°C), US zones

7–10. A hybrid raised in Holland in the 20th century.

Rhododendron schlippenbachii
A deciduous azalea that grows to 16ft (4.5m) tall, bearing thin leaves 2–3½in (5–9cm) long and producing trusses of 3–6 flat pink or white flowers 1¼–2in (3–5cm) across, spotted reddish-pink on the upper lobes, in May to June. Hardy to −20°F (−29°C), US zones 5–9. Native to Korea and NE China.

Rhododendron schlippenbachii

Flowering Dogwood *Cornus florida*

Weigela florida 'Foliis Purpureis'

Cornus

Flowering Dogwood *Cornus florida*   This large deciduous shrub or small tree grows to 30ft (9m) tall, producing insignificant green flowers with yellow tops, framed by four attractive white or pink bracts, between April and June. Superb autumn colour, particularly after a good summer. Hardy to −20°F (−29°C), US zones 5–9. Native to eastern USA in deciduous woods and fields.

PLANTING HELP   Prefers acid soil and light shade. Does not thrive on chalk.

Weigela

Weigela florida **'Foliis Purpureis'**   A compact deciduous shrub that grows up to 5ft (1.5m) tall, bearing clusters of funnel-shaped deep rosy pink flowers 1½in (4cm) long and pale or white within the tube, in early summer. The leaves are narrowly oval, about 2–3in (5–8cm) long and purple-tinged or brownish-green. The unusual leaf colour sets off the flowers rather attractively but needs brighter silvery or yellow foliage nearby to lighten the effect later in the year. Hardy to −10°F (−23°C), US zones 6–9. *Weigela florida* is native to China, Korea and S Japan, and while the origin of 'Foliis Purpureis' is uncertain, it came into commerce in the early 20th century.

PLANTING HELP   Plant in autumn or spring in any soil in sun or partial shade. No regular pruning is required other than the occasional pruning out of old and weak wood.

Halesia

Mountain Snowdrop Tree *Halesia monticola*
A deciduous tree that grows to 80ft (25m) tall, although it usually attains only 30ft (9m) in gardens. In late spring, leaves emerge 2–5in (5–12cm) long; the branches are wreathed in clusters of small white bell-shaped flowers to 1in (2.5cm) long, followed by curious, hard, 4-winged fruits 2in (5cm) long. Hardy to −20°F (−29°C), US zones 5–9. Native to SE North America. This tree flowers best in areas with a definite cool winter period.

PLANTING HELP   Plant in autumn or early spring in fairly moist well-drained acid or neutral soil in sun or partial shade. No regular pruning is needed but young trees may need to be kept to a single leading shoot, unless a bush rather than a tree is desired.

Viburnum

Attractive for their clusters of sometimes fragrant white, cream or pink flowers, as well as for their foliage and berries, viburnums can be evergreen, semi-evergreen or deciduous shrubs or trees. The leaves of the deciduous varieties sometimes colour well in autumn. Native to the woods of many temperate regions but also to South America and SE Asia.

PLANTING HELP   Plant in moist, well-drained, fertile soil in sun or partial shade; it is best to plant several of the same species together to ensure the production of fruit. Sow seed in autumn or take cuttings in summer. Eating the fruit can cause illness.

Viburnum plicatum 'Mariesii'   A spreading deciduous shrub that grows to 7ft (2m) tall, the shoots arranged horizontally, producing a beautiful layered effect. The leaves 2½–4in (6–10cm) long; the flowers produced in flat heads along the branches in May. Hardy to –20°F (–29°C), US zones 5–9. Native to both Japan and China.

Guelder Rose *Viburnum opulus* 'Sterile' A deciduous shrub that grows to 12ft (3.5m) tall and about as wide. In early summer it bears rounded clusters up to 2½in (6cm) wide, of sterile flowers ¾in (2cm) wide. The maple-like,

three-lobed leaves are up to 4in (10cm) long and usually turn purple and deep red in autumn. Hardy to –20°F (–29°C), US zones 5–9. The species *V. opulus* with flat flower heads, is native to Europe, W Asia and N Africa, and has long been cultivated.

Guelder Rose

Viburnum plicatum 'Mariesii'

Mountain Snowdrop Tree *Halesia monticola*

Tricyrtis

Tricyrtis hirta Elegant clumps of ascending
and arching stems 16–35in (40–80cm) long, bear
leaves 3–6in (8–15cm) long, and produce nearly
white, subtle rather than showy flowers from July
to September; because of their spotted flowers
Tricyrtis are called **Toad Lilies**. Hardy to 0°F
(−18°C), US zones 7–10. Native to Japan, growing
on shady rocks.

PLANTING HELP For moist leafy soil in
partial shade and shelter. Soil must be kept moist.
Sow seed when ripe and divide plants in spring.
Slugs and snails may attack young plants.

Dianella

Dianella tasmanica A perennial forming
clumps of stiff leaves with rough edges that grows
to 4ft (1.2m) tall and 1in (2.5cm) wide, bearing
stems 5ft (1.5m) long, which produce a profusion
of star-shaped pale blue flowers in branching
sprays from August to October. Hardy to 10°F
(−12°C), US zones 8–10. Native to Tasmania
and SE Australia, growing in cool, damp,
shady forests.

PLANTING HELP Plant in moist lime-free
peaty soil in a sheltered position in shade. Keep
moist in winter. Sow seed or divide in spring.

Disporum

Fairy Bells *Disporum sessile* 'Variegatum'
A woodland perennial forming colonies of stems
1–2ft (30–60cm) tall, bearing very attractive
striped leaves and producing greenish white
flowers 1in (2.5cm) long, from April to May. Blue

Tricyrtis hirta

Fairy Bells *Disporum sessile* 'Variegatum'

Dianella tasmanica

Lily-of-the-valley *Convallaria majalis*

black berries. Hardy to 0°F (−18°C), US zones 7–10. The wild green form is native to Japan, growing in woods in the hills.

PLANTING HELP   For moist, fertile, leafy soil in partial shade, although *D. smithii* (*not shown*) will thrive in deep shade. Sow seed in autumn or divide in spring; these plants sometimes seed themselves, especially in shade.

Lily-of-the-valley

Convallaria majalis   A favourite in cottage gardens, this herbaceous perennial grows to 8in (20cm) tall and spreads vigorously to form extensive colonies. In late spring it produces erect stems bearing a pair of leaves, each 8in (20cm) long, and a spike of small, bell-shaped, heavily scented white flowers ⅓in (1cm) long. The fruit is a small shiny red berry which is poisonous when eaten. Hardy to −10°F (−23°C), US zones 6–9. Native to Europe, E North America and NE Asia. Excellent ground-cover in shady places, particularly beneath rhododendrons.

PLANTING HELP   Plant in autumn or early spring in moist fertile soil in full or partial shade. Divide in autumn. Top dress regularly with leafmould. The flowers are rather hidden by the leaves, but lovely to pick and bring indoors.

Liriope

Liriope muscari
An evergreen perennial that grows to 1ft (30cm) tall, forming dense grassy clumps, making good ground-cover under trees or around shrubs in hot areas. In autumn it produces stiff spikes of small light violet flowers, each about ½in (1.5cm) wide. The leathery arching leaves are 18in (45cm) long; the berry-like fruit is small and black. Hardy to 10°F (−12°C), US zones 8–10. Native to China and Japan and introduced into cultivation in the 19th century.

Liriope muscari

PLANTING HELP   Plant in autumn or spring in any leafy soil in a partially shaded or sunny position. Sow seed or divide in spring. Young plants may be eaten by slugs.

Corydalis

The name corydalis is derived from the Greek word *korudallis* meaning 'crested lark', which was thought to resemble the flower shape of these small perennials, attractive for both flowers and foliage. There are many different species of corydalis, some preferring full sun, and others happiest in some shade. Easily grown and self-seeding, particularly in shady crevices in walls and among rocks.

Corydalis flexuosa 'China Blue'

PLANTING HELP   Plant in well-drained moist leafy soil. *C. flexuosa* and *C. lutea* should always be planted in shade or partial shade, whereas *C. ochroleuca* can be planted in sun or shade, although it will remain in flower for longer in shade. Self-seeds freely. Plants can be divided in autumn. Slugs and snails can be a problem.

Corydalis flexuosa **'China Blue'** An herbaceous perennial that grows to 16in (40cm) tall, spreading by stolons to form extensive patches, producing clusters of blue or sometimes mauve blue flowers, about 1in (2.5cm) long, over a long period in spring and early summer. Delicate fleshy leaves sometimes marked purple, emerge in autumn. Hardy to −10°F (−23°C), US zones 6–9. Native to W China, growing on shady slopes.

Corydalis lutea   This easily grown plant forms a mound of delicate green leaves, producing stems to 15in (40cm) long and bearing clusters of yellow flowers from May to October. Hardy to −10°F (−23°C), US zones 6–9. Native to the foothills of the Alps in Switzerland, Italy and the former Yugoslavia, growing on shady rocks and screes, and frequently naturalized elsewhere.

Corydalis ochroleuca (syn. *Pseudofumaria alba*) A bushy perennial with erect stems to 16in (40cm) long, from a central rootstock, bearing clusters of 14 creamy white flowers, each about ⅔in (2cm) long, from May to September. For sun or shade. Hardy to 0°F (−18°C), US zones 7–10. Native to SE Europe and naturalized elsewhere in Europe, growing in rocky woods and especially growing on walls or crevices in pavement.

Corydalis ochroleuca

Geranium nodosum

Corydalis lutea

AlbumWood Cranesbill *Geranium sylvaticum*

Geranium endressii

Dusky Cranesbill *Geranium phaeum*

Cranesbill

These amazingly versatile, easily grown plants are, in our opinion, an absolute must for any garden. Most will grow in sun or partial shade, although a few, *G. nodosum* and *G. phaeum* (*shown here*) actually prefer complete shade in hot areas. They will quickly fill an empty patch and can provide interest for most of the year.

PLANTING HELP   Plant in sun or partial shade, in moderately fertile well-drained soil; these plants will not tolerate boggy conditions. Water regularly during flowering and feed monthly with a liquid fertilizer. Sow seed or divide clumps in spring; geraniums can also be propagated by taking cuttings below lowest leaves.

Geranium nodosum   Although unspectacular, this plant will tolerate the densest driest shade, forming spreading patches which produce bluish or purplish flowers 1in (2.5cm) wide, from June to October. A hardy and modest plant for a wild garden, valuable for its late-flowering in hot weather. Hardy to 0°F (−18°C), US zones 7–10. Native of the Pyrenees eastwards to Italy and the former Yugoslavia, growing in the woods in the mountains and hills.

Wood Cranesbill *Geranium sylvaticum*
Stems to 2¼ft (70cm) bearing upward-facing purplish-blue flowers ¾–1in (2–2.5cm) wide, from May to July. Hardy to −10°F (−23°C), US zones 6–9 or less. Native to Europe, growing in grassy places, by roads and rivers and in open woods. 'Album' has white flowers.

Geranium endressii   An evergreen plant which forms large patches, providing excellent ground-cover, and seems to produce pretty pink flowers throughout the summer. Hardy to 0°F (−18°C), US zones 7–10. Native to SW France and NW Spain in the western end of the Pyrenees, growing in damp places in the wild.

Dusky Cranesbill, **Mourning Widow** *Geranium phaeum*   An herbaceous perennial that grows to 2ft (60cm) tall, forming clumps of foliage that bears many almost black, deep maroon or purplish flat flowers 1in (2.5cm) wide, on erect stems in summer. Hardy to −10°F (−23°C), US zones 6–9, or lower. Native to much of Europe. A most useful plant for really shady places, being quite drought-tolerant once established.
Geranium phaeum 'Album' Has white flowers.

Eomecon chionantha

Meconopsis grandis

Eomecon

Eomecon chionantha   Easily grown in moist leafy soil, this perennial forms wide mats of large round leaves and produces flower stems to 16in (40cm) high, bearing white flowers with yellow centres 1½in (4cm) across, from April to July. Hardy to −10°F (−23°C), US zones 6–9. Native to E China, growing on the banks of the Bamboo River, presumably under trees.

PLANTING HELP   Be careful! This plant can become invasive if it grows well, although it dislikes drought and cold.

Meconopsis

Although the more traditional red poppies, *Papaver*, require full sun, their cousins, the *Meconopsis* will do well in partial shade. The blue Himalayan poppy was first exhibited at the Chelsea Flower Show in 1926 and caused a sensation, although, in fact, *Meconopsis betonicifolia* had been discovered by Abbé Delavay a few years previously. Despite being short-lived and tempermental, the pleasure of watching poppies unravel like crushed silk to display their almost translucent petals is worth the effort of growing them.

PLANTING HELP   *Meconopsis* plants prefer cool damp summers. They should be planted in a sandy peaty soil, partially shaded, sheltered from the wind and kept moist. Seed should be spread thinly in loamless seed compost and given plenty of moisture; damp rather than wet conditions provide the greatest chance of successful growth. Plant clumps can be divided. Problems can arise from mildew, slugs and snails.

Himalyan Blue Poppy *Meconopsis betonicifolia* (syn. *M. baileyi*)   An herbaceous biennial or perennial that grows to 4ft (1.2m) tall, producing blue flowers 4in (10cm) wide, in early summer. Hardy to 0°F (−18°C), US zones 7–10. Native to Burma and W China, growing in woods and along streams in alpine meadows. This plant sometimes dies after flowering but if prevented from seeding may survive for a second or third year.

Meconopsis quintuplinervia   This plant forms extensive clumps, bearing leaves 10in (25cm) long and flower stems up to 3ft (90cm) tall, although not usually more than 1ft (30cm) tall. The singly borne, pinkish to azure blue flowers, have petals 1½in (4cm) wide and appear from June to August. Hardy to −10°F (−23°C), US zones 6–9. Native to C and W China growing in alpine

Welsh Poppy at Tintinhull House, Somerset, England

Meconopsis villosa

Welsh Poppy

Himalyan Blue Poppy

Meconopsis quintuplinervia

meadows on limestone, often among dwarf *Rhododendron* scrub.

Welsh Poppy *Meconopsis cambrica*
An herbaceous perennial that grows to 2ft (60cm) tall, producing a succession of solitary yellow flowers 2½in (6cm) wide, in summer. Self-seeds and spreads rapidly. Hardy to −10°F (−23°C), US zones 6–9. Native to W Europe.

Meconopsis grandis This plant forms large clumps of stems to 4ft (1.2m) tall, bearing between 1 and 4 flowers of often purplish petals 1½in (4cm) wide, from June to August. Hardy to

−10°F (−23°C), US zones 6–9. Native to N India and Nepal to SW China, growing on rocky hillsides and in scrub. Reputed to be grown around shepherds' huts in N India where the seeds are used for oil.

Meconopsis villosa An easily grown plant for a shaded sheltered position, although it can be damaged by warm wet weather in winter. Stems 2–5ft (60–150cm), bearing between 1 and 5 yellow flowers with petals 1in (2.5cm) wide, from May to July. Hardy to 0°F (−18°C), US zones 7–10. Native to the Himalayas on shady rocks and by streams in forest and forest clearings.

Mitella breweri

Pick-a-back plant *Tolmiea menziesii*

Mitella

Mitella breweri An easily grown evergreen with trailing flowering stems 4–12in (10–30cm) tall, bearing clusters of tiny greenish-yellow flowers in early summer. Leaves ¼in (1.5cm) long. Hardy to −10°F (−23°C), US zones 6–9. Native to central California, north to British Columbia and Montana, growing on damp shady slopes in conifer forest.

PLANTING HELP For shady leafy soil. Sow seeds or divide in spring. Slugs and snails are attracted to this plant.

Pick-a-back plant

Youth-on-age *Tolmiea menziesii* A fast spreading herbaceous perennial forming large clumps, bearing flowering stems 12–27in (30–80cm) long. Hardy to 0°F (−19°C), US zones 7–10. Native to western North America from northern California to Alaska, growing in coniferous forest in cool shady places.

PLANTING HELP For shade or partial shade. Propagation by division in spring or by planting out the baby (pick-a-back) plantlets that form at the base of the mature leaves. This plant makes the very best shade ground-cover we know. Free from pests and diseases.

Tiarella

Foam Flower *Tiarella cordifolia* Plants forming large spreading mats by creeping underground stolons. Leaves 2–4in (5–10cm) long with scattered hairs and attractive autumn colour. Flowers ½in (1.5cm) across. Hardy to 0°F (−18°C), US zones 7–10. Native of E North America from Nova Scotia to Ontario and Minnesota, growing in woods in the mountains.

Foam Flower *Tiarella cordifolia*

Heuchera 'Palace Purple'

Heuchera cylindrica 'Greenfinch'

Saxifraga fortunei

PLANTING HELP   Plant in cool, moist, fertile soil in shade. Sow seeds or divide in spring. Slugs love to eat the leaves of this plant.

Heuchera

These evergreen or semi-evergreen perennials from North America have woody roots which spread slowly into large clumps, providing good ground-cover; the tiny bell-shaped flowers rise on stems well above the circular leaves which are hairy and sometimes beautifully tinted with grey.

PLANTING HELP   Plant in well-drained fertile soil in full sun or partial shade, sinking roots well into the ground so that only the top of the foliage is visible. It is a good idea to divide and replant *Heuchera* every few years, preferably in August or early September. Regular feeding will ensure a proliferation of flowers in May and June, continuing into the autumn.

Heuchera cylindrica   Plant forming mats of heart-shaped, dark green, wavy edged leaves 1–3in (2.5–8cm) wide and stems 6–36in (15–90cm) long, bearing insignificant cream or greenish-yellow flowers in spring and summer. Hardy to −10°F (−23°C), US zones 6–9. The variety **'Greenfinch'** has green flowers.

Heuchera **'Palace Purple'**   A perennial that forms mounds of striking leaves 8in (20cm) tall, purplish-black with a metallic sheen. Those produced in winter are nearly round whereas summer leaves are divided. It had masses of minute white flowers. Hardy to −20°F (−29°C), US zones 5–9.

Saxifrage

Saxifraga fortunei   A deciduous or evergreen plant forming small clumps to 1ft (30cm) tall and wide. Fleshy leaves 1½–8in (4–20cm) wide. Stems 2–18in (5–45cm) tall, producing white flowers from July to October. Hardy to 0°F (−18°C), US zones 7–10. Native to Japan, Korea, E Siberia and N China, growing on wet shaded rocks by streams in the mountains and to sea level in the north.

PLANTING HELP   For moist fertile soil in shade. Sow seeds in autumn or divide in spring. Insects and slugs may cause problems.

Cimicifuga rubifolia

Cimicifuga

Cimicifuga rubifolia An herbaceous perennial that grows to 6ft (1.8m) tall, forming clumps and producing erect branched clusters up to 2ft (60cm) long, with many small creamy white flowers, in summer. The leaves are divided into nine or more oval leaflets, each about 4in (10cm) long. Hardy to −10°F (−23°C), US zones 6–9. Native to E North America. *Cimicifuga simplex* is a most attractive late-flowering plant, often with deep purple leaves 'Atropurpurea' contrasting with the fluffy spikes of creamy flowers.

PLANTING HELP   Plant in moist rich soil in autumn or spring in shade or partial shade. Propagate by division in spring.

Creeping Jenny *Lysimachia nummularia* 'Aurea'

Creeping Jenny

Moneywort *Lysimachia nummularia* 'Aurea' An evergreen perennial herb with a distinct leaf shape and colour which contrasts beautifully with other shade-loving foliage plants. Creeping stems to 2¼ft (70cm) or more long, bear bright yellowish-green leaves, and yellow cup-shaped flowers on short stalks are produced from April to September. Hardy to −10°F (−23°C), US zones 6–9. The wild green-leaved form is native to most of Europe, E to Russia and naturalized in North America, growing in damp woods, fens and on the banks of streams and lake shores. Herbalists of old thought this was one of the most effective herbs in the treatment of wounds; a ointment or compress made from fresh leaves was applied externally to wounds, whereas drinking an infusion of fresh leaves was thought to alleviate internal bleeding.

PLANTING HELP   Plant in moist fertile soil in partial shade and propagate by division in spring or autumn. Slugs and snails can cause problems.

Beetleweed *Galax urceolata*

Doronicum

Leopard's Bane *Doronicum* These easily grown deciduous perennials produce bright yellow daisy-like flowers just as the daffodils begin to fade in spring, ensuring a continuation of yellow hues in the spring garden.

PLANTING HELP   Plant in any fertile soil in partial shade. *Doronicum orientale* is tolerant of drought in summer when the leaves have died down, but can suffer from root rot if the soil is too wet. Sow seed in spring or divide in early autumn. Problems may arise from mildew and leaf spot.

Doronicum orientale (syn. *D. caucasicum*)
A perennial spreading slowly to make wide patches, bearing solitary flower heads 1–2in (2.5–5cm) wide, from March to May, on stalks that can reach 2–3ft (60–90cm) tall, although they are usually around 1ft (30cm) tall. Hardy to 0°F (–18°C), US zones 7–10. Native to SE Europe, east to Hungary and the Caucasus, and south to Turkey and Lebanon, growing in woods and scrub.

Great Leopard's Bane
Doronicum pardalianches
A plant forming spreading patches with stems to 3ft (90cm) tall, bearing between 2 and 6 flowers, 1–2in (2.5–5cm) across from May to July. Can be invasive. Hardy to –10°F (–23°C), US zones 6–9. Native to the mainland of W Europe , Austria and the Czech and Slovak republics, in woods. Naturalized in Britain

Great
Leopard's Bane

Doronicum orientale

Galax

Beetleweed *Galax urceolata* (syn. *G aphylla*)
An evergreen plant forming mats of shiny leathery leaves 1–6in (3–15cm) wide, which take on copper tints in autumn. Flowering stems to 2¾ft (80cm) long, bear tiny white flowers ¼in (0.5cm) wide, in midsummer. Hardy to –10°F (–23°C), US zones 6–9. Native to E North America, growing in dry open woods, mainly in mountains. For leafy lime-free soil in shade or partial shade.

PLANTING HELP   Seeds should be planted in ericaceous (lime-free) compost. Alternatively, propagate by division early in spring. Slugs and snails can cause problems.

Silphium

Silphium perfoliatum   A tall leafy perennial forming clumps which produce stems to 8ft (2.5m) tall, bearing yellow daisies 2–2¾in (5–7cm) across, from July to September. Hardy to –20°F (–29°C), US zones 5–9. Native of E North America from Ontario to S Dakota, south to Georgia, Missouri and Oklahoma.

PLANTING HELP   Growing in damp woods, on riverbanks, in scrub and moist meadows. For rich moist soil in sun or shade.

Silphium perfoliatum

Hosta 'Royal Standard'

Hosta sieboldiana 'Frances Williams'

Hostas

Hosta sieboldiana

Hostas are perennial plants that form slowly increasing clumps of broad striking foliage in a diversity of sizes, shapes, textures and colours. They are easy to grow, thriving in damp or fairly dry soil, in dense or partial shade, or in full sun if kept well watered, associating well with most other shade plants. They are not bothered by insects but slugs and snails can be a problem. The leaves are at their best in late spring; hostas remain attractive however, providing excellent ground-cover and the flowers on arching spikes in summer keep up the interest. The dying leaves brighten up the dreary, late autumn garden with creams and yellows. Few other perennials repay initial planting efforts so well; they are long-lived, multiplying faithfully and in most cases quite rapidly.

Hosta 'Halcyon'

Hostas in a garden in Oldwick, New Jersey   Hosta 'Krossa Regal'

PLANTING HELP   Plant in early spring or late summer in ordinary garden soil. If possible, prepare the site a month in advance by lining a deep hole with a layer of well-rotted farmyard manure or garden compost and cover with earth mixed with fine leaf mould. If planting in hot summer weather, the hosta must be thoroughly watered-in; large varieties will need water every day for at least a week, preferably morning and evening. The site should then be surrounded with a ring of mulching material. Regular fertilizing or feeding is beneficial and will be reflected in the appearance of the plant. When the plant is four or five years old, it can be split by putting two garden forks into the centre of the roots and pulling; it requires some effort but the result is two beautiful plants for the price of one! The empty space which the hosta's leaves cover in summer is an ideal habitat for early-flowering bulbs such as Snowdrops, Aconites and Glory-of-the-Snow.

Hosta **'Halcyon'**   Grows to 20in (50cm) tall and 3ft (90cm) wide, bearing blue-green/grey leaves 7in × 4in (18cm × 10cm) and producing bell-shaped violet flowers in midsummer. Best in full shade; its colour fades in too much sun. Hardy to −40°F (−40°C), US zones 3–8. One of the Tardiana group of hostas of which *H. sieboldiana* is a parent.

Hosta **'Krossa Regal'**   Superb in leaf and flower, producing upright greyish-blue leaves and orchid pink, bell-shaped flowers in late summer. Hardy to −40°F (−40°C), US zones 3–8. Native to Japan and imported into the USA as a seedling by

Gus Krossa, one of the first American Hosta collectors.

Hosta **'Royal Standard'** (syn. *H.* 'Wayside Perfection')   This cultivar forms a mound to 2ft (60cm) tall and 15in (40cm) wide of heart-shaped leaves 10 × 7in (26 × 18cm), producing fragrant white funnel-shaped flowers in late summer. Rapid and vigorous growth make this an excellent ground-cover or landscaping plant. Shade to three-quarters sun. Hardy to −40°F (−40°C), US zones 3–8. A hybrid between *Hosta plantaginea* and possibly *Hosta sieboldii*.

Hosta sieboldiana   One of the commonest hostas in the wild, this plant forms a magnificent clump of heavily puckered, sumptuous, blue-grey green leaves 12 × 14in (30 × 35cm), often too large for today's small garden. White flowers tinged with violet emerge on short stems in July and the seed heads remain intact after the leaves collapse, providing interest in winter. Shade to three-quarters sun. Hardy to −40°F (−40°C), US zones 3–8. Native to Japan.

Hosta sieboldiana **'Frances Williams'**   Puckered bluish-green leaves with wide, irregular, yellowish margins 14 × 6in (36 × 20cm) form a mound 2½ft (75cm) high; pale lavender flowers are produced in July. Shade to half-shade. Resistant to slug and snail damage, but it takes at least four years to establish. Hardy to −40°F (−40°C), US zones 3–8. Sport of *Hosta sieboldiana* 'Elegans'.

Hosta fortunei 'Aureo-marginata'

Hosta undulata var. *univitatta*

Hosta undulata
var. *univitatta*

Hosta undulata var. univitatta
Reaching 18in (45cm) tall, this plant bears small leaves 1½in (4cm) wide, with a white striped centre surrounded by blue-green and twisted towards the tips. Shade to half sun. Flowers rich lilac in July. Vulnerable to slug and snail damage. Hardy to −40°F (−40°C), US zones 3–8. Native to Japan.

Hosta fortunei 'Aureo-marginata' Grows to about 14in (35cm) tall and 2ft (60cm) wide, bearing dark green leaves with distinct, wide, golden edges and violet flowers in midsummer. Shade to three-quarters sun. Hardy to −40°F (−40°C), US zones 3–8. Probably of garden origin.

Hosta undulata 'Albomarginata' (syn. *Hosta* 'Thomas Hogg') Grows to 1½ft (45cm) tall and 3ft (90cm) wide, bearing funnel-shaped lilac flowers in midsummer. The leaves are green with an irregular creamy-white margin, 8 × 3in (20 × 8cm) in size. Grows in shade to half-sun. Vulnerable to slug and snail damage Hardy to −40°F (−40°C), US zones 3–8. Brought from Japan to USA by Thomas Hogg in 1875.

Hosta ventricosa Growing up to 14in (35cm) tall and 2ft (60cm) wide, this plant produces deep lilac mauve flowers up to 3in (8cm) wide, in late summer. The leaves are heart-shaped dark green above and mid- to dark green beneath, 7 × 5in (18 × 12cm). Shade to half-shade but vulnerable to slug and snail damage. Hardy to −40°F (−40°C), US zones 3–8. Native to China.

Hosta ventricosa 'Aureomaculata' (syn. *Hosta ventricosa* 'Maculata') Bearing leaves with a yellowish-green centre and a dark green margin that become a uniform dark green in summer, this plant bears violet flowers in August. Shade to half-shade. Vulnerable to slug and snail damage. Hardy

Hosta 'Shade Fanfare'

Hosta 'Ginko Craig'

Hosta ventricosa 'Aureomaculata'

Hosta ventricosa

to −40°F (−40°C), US zones 3–8. Native to China and N Korea.

***Hosta* 'Ginko Craig'** Grows to 4in (10cm) tall and 10in (25cm) wide if divided to keep the juvenile form, or three times bigger if allowed to mature. The leaves are medium to dark green with clear white margins, and purple-striped flowers emerge in midsummer. Hardy to −40°F (−40°C), US zones 3–8. Introduced by Alex Craig-Summers who reputedly found it in a Japanese market and named it for his Japanese wife.

***Hosta* 'Shade Fanfare'** This fast-growing hosta reaches 18in (45cm) tall and 2ft (60cm) wide, with leaves 8 × 6in (20 × 15cm) varying from light green to yellow, edged with a cream margin. The funnel-shaped flowers are lavender and bloom in midsummer. Shade to full sun. Hardy to −40°F (−40°C), US zones 3–8. Derived from *Hosta* 'Flamboyant'.

Hosta undulata 'Albomarginata'

69

Hosta 'Wide Brim'

Hosta 'Gold Edger'

Hosta 'Honeybells'

Hosta **'August Moon'** This fast-growing hosta produces a medium to large vigorous clump of leaves that unfurl pale green and gradually become pale gold. Pale lavender flowers emerge in midsummer. Vulnerable to slug and snail damage. Of unknown origin, this plant was found in a garden in New York in the 1960s.

Hosta **'Gold Standard'**
To 2ft (60cm) tall and 3¼ft (95cm) wide, bearing yellow leaves 3 × 5in (8 × 13cm) with green edges, and pale lavender flowers in midsummer. This is a fast-growing hosta that gives the best colour when mature. A quarter to three-quarters sun. Hardy to−40°F (−40°C), US zones 3–8. Introduced by Pauline Banyai in 1976.

Hosta 'Gold Standard'

Hosta 'Gold Standard'

Hosta 'August Moon'

Hosta 'Gold Edger' True to its name, this is an excellent hosta for edging or placing at the front of a border. It produces golden-yellow leaves 4 × 3in (10 × 7½cm) which increase rapidly to provide dense ground-cover, and bear masses of lavender flowers in midsummer. Resistant to slug and snail damage. Hardy to −40°F (−40°C), US zones 3–8. A cultivar raised by Paul Aden in USA.

Hosta 'Honeybells' This rapidly growing hosta is excellent for covering large areas of ground. It bears pointed, light green leaves with wavy edges and produces sweetly scented white flowers streaked with violet in late summer. Hardy to −40°F (−40°C), US zones 3–8. Thought to be a hybrid between *H. plantaginea* and possibly *H. sieboldii*.

Hosta 'Wide Brim' Grows to 20in (50cm) tall and 3ft (90cm) wide, bearing wide green leaves with yellow margins turning whitish and producing funnel-shaped pale lavender flowers in midsummer. Shade to three-quarters sun. Hardy to −40°F (−40°C), US zones 3–8. A cultivar developed by crossing *Hosta* 'Bold One' with *Hosta* 'Bold Ribbons'.

Hosta 'Zounds' Grows to 20in (50cm) tall and 2½ft (75cm) wide, this plant bears puckered, golden-metallic leaves 8 × 7in (20 × 18cm) and funnel-shaped, pale lavender flowers in midsummer. A quarter to three-quarters sun. Resistant to slug and snail damage. Hardy to −40°F (−40°C), US zones 3–8. A cultivar developed from a *Hosta sieboldiana* 'Elegans' hybrid.

Hosta 'Zounds'

Campanula takesimana

Platycodon grandiflorus

Sweet Woodruff

Campanula latifolia

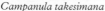

Willow Gentian *Gentiana asclepiadea*

Campanula

Campanulas are recognized by their bell-shaped flowers, usually in some shade of blue. They will all tolerate some shade and choice will depend on the situation. They are easy to grow and flower over a long period.

PLANTING HELP   For moist, fertile, well-drained soil in sun or partial shade; the flowers do better in shade. Divide in spring or autumn. Attractive to slugs and snails.

Campanula latifolia   A perennial with upright stems to 3½ft (1m) tall, producing blue flowers in summer. Hardy to −20°F (−29°C), US zones 5–9. Native to most of Europe and parts of Asia, growing in hedges, scrub, forests and meadows, often on limestone. There is a white flowered form which is especially beautiful.

Campanula takesimana   A perennial that reaches 2ft (60cm) tall, the bottom leaves forming rosettes. Beautiful pale blue or pink flowers, spotted maroon inside, about 2in (5cm) long, are produced throughout the summer. Hardy to −20°F (−29°C), US zones 5–9. Native to Korea and introduced into cultivation in the late 20th century.

Foxglove

Common Foxglove *Digitalis purpurea*
An herbaceous biennial or perennial that forms clumps to 7ft (2m) tall, and produces bell-shaped purplish-pink flowers, each about 2in (5cm) long, in summer. Hardy to −20°F (−29°C), US zones

Common Foxglove *Digitalis purpurea* in Wales   Common Foxglove

5–9. Native to most of Europe and naturalised in North America. In the late 18th century *Digitalis purpurea* was discovered to be a treatment for heart problems, and modern research has confirmed its efficacy. However, it is poisonous in overdose. The white form is especially beautiful, but needs to be kept separate from the pink if it is to come true from seed.

PLANTING HELP   Plant in light well-drained soil in partial shade. The seed should be sown in April; it will produce leaves in the first year and flowers in the second. A great favourite with bees and small insects.

Gentiana

Willow Gentian *Gentiana asclepiadea*
A perennial that grows to 2ft (60cm) tall. In late summer it bears blue or rarely white flowers about 2in (5cm) long. Hardy to −10°F (−23°C), US zones 6–9. Willow Gention is native to the mountainous areas of Europe.

PLANTING HELP   Plant in autumn or spring in any fertile, moist soil in a partially shaded position. Divide in spring. Slugs and snails may be a problem, eating the young shoots as they emerge in spring.

Platycodon

Platycodon grandiflorus   A perennial with stems to 1¼–3½ft (40–100cm) tall, producing blue flowers 1½in (4cm) wide in late summer. Hardy to −10°F (−23°C), US zones 6–9. Native to

Japan, Korea, N China and E Siberia, growing on grassy slopes in hills and mountains.

PLANTING HELP   Plant in moist fertile soil in sun or partial shade. Divide in summer. Slugs and snails are attracted to the young shoots.

Sweet Woodruff

Galium odoratum (syn. *Asperula odorata*)
A perennial herb with erect stems to 9in (23cm) tall, making attractive ground-cover. In spring and early summer it produces loose heads of small white flowers, each about ¼in (0.5cm) wide. For shade and partial shade. Hardy to −20°F (−29°C), US zones 5–9. Native to N and C Europe, south to North Africa and east to Siberia. In the Middle Ages Sweet Woodruff was valued for its smell and used to ward off moths and insects. It also had several medicinal uses and the dried plant was used to make a tea, said to have a soothing and tranquilizing effect. To this day in Germany, it is steeped in Rhine wine to make a delightful drink known as the *Maibowle* which is drunk on the first of May.

Sweet Woodruff

PLANTING HELP
The plant is sometimes slow to establish, so it is worth planting as large a plant as possible; ideally beg a big chunk from a friend.

73

Lady's Mantle *Alchemilla mollis*

Bunchberry *Cornus canadensis*

Synthyris stellata

Anemonopsis

Anemonopsis macrophylla A clump-forming perennial with a thick rootstock and upright stems to 2½ft (75cm) tall, bearing divided leaves and producing nodding flowers 1–1¾in (2.5–4.5cm) from July to September. Hardy to 0°F (−18°C), US zones 7–10. Native to the mountainous woods of Japan.

PLANTING HELP   Plant in moist, fertile, acid soil in shade and protect from cold winds. Sow seed or divide in spring. Needs cool shade.

Asarina

Asarina procumbens A drought-tolerant perennial that grows to 3in (8cm) tall with trailing stems to 1ft (30cm) long or more. For several months in the summer it produces its snapdragon-like flowers 1½in (4cm) long, pale creamy yellow with an orange throat. The clammily hairy leaves are rounded or kidney-shaped and slightly divided. Hardy to 10°F (−12°C), US zones 8–10. Native to SW Europe and introduced into cultivation in the 19th century. This plant is a quietly attractive ground-cover for a dry shady place, thriving under trees and shrubs.

PLANTING HELP   Plant in autumn or early spring in any well-drained soil, in a partially shaded sheltered position.

Bunchberry

Cornus canadensis (syn. *Chamaepericlymenum canadense*)   A perennial forming patches a number of feet across, bearing flowering stems 2¾–8in (7–20cm) tall, with leaves in a whorl and tiny green flowers produced from May to July. The fruits are bright red and fleshy. Hardy to 0°F (−18°C), US zones 7–10. Native to North America, Japan, Korea and E Siberia, growing in coniferous woods.

PLANTING HELP   Easily grown in moist acid soil in shade or partial shade. Sow seed in autumn. Divide in spring or autumn.

Lady's Mantle

Alchemilla mollis The name *Alchemilla* is derived from the Arabic *alchimia* meaning 'alchemy', and originated from alchemists' belief that the plant has miraculous properties. An herbaceous perennial herb that grows to 18in (45cm) tall, producing airy sprays of tiny yellow flowers held well above the foliage in summer. The

Asarina procumbens   *Houttuynia cordata*   *Houttuynia cordata* 'Variegata'

softly hairy grey-green leaves are rounded, up to 6in (15cm) long. Hardy to −10°F (−23°C), US zones 6–9. Native to E Europe and W Asia and introduced into cultivation in the 19th century. This plant is greatly cherished for its fine foliage, seen at its best after a shower when the hairs trap many glistening raindrops. It has an informal 'cottage garden' look that associates well with a wide range of other plants.

PLANTING HELP   Plant in autumn or early spring in any soil in sun or partial shade. As it may self-seed freely, it is often wise to cut off the flower heads as they start to turn brown. It is quite drought tolerant. Slugs and snails may eat the young leaves.

Houttuynia

Marsh plants that will succeed in any cool, fairly moist border where they will creep freely underground. *Houttuynia cordata* is very invasive although its cultivars are less vigorous. One of its type is a perennial useful for ground-cover in damp situation.

Houttuynia cordata   An herbaceous perennial that grows to 18in (45cm) tall, spreading into patches much wider than tall. In summer it produces solitary white flowers 1in (2.5cm) wide, with four or more white petal-like bracts surrounding a yellow green cone. The leaves to 2in (5cm) long, are elegant heart-shaped and smell a bit like Seville oranges. Hardy to 0°F (−18°C), US zones 7–10. Native to Japan, China and the Himalayas, growing in damp shady places, woods and scrub. The leaves can be eaten like spinach, and are much collected in the mountains of W China and sold in local markets. They have a strong ginger-like flavour.
Houttuynia cordata 'Variegata'

(syn. *Houttuynia cordata* 'Chameleon')   Broadly heart-shaped and heavily variegated with cream and crimson.

PLANTING HELP   Plant in autumn or early spring, in any soil in sun or shade. However it is important to maintain moist conditions.

Synthyris

Synthyris stellata (syn. *Synthyris missurica*) A perennial with stems to 2ft (60cm) tall, bearing jagged-edged leaves 1–3in (2.5–8cm) across and producing clusters of purple flowers ¼–⅓in (0.5–1cm) long, from April to July. Hardy to −10°F (−23°C), US zones 6–9. Native to W North America, growing in moist places in the mountains and foothills.

PLANTING HELP   Plant in moist soil in a cool position, but do not allow soil to become wet. For partial or total shade. Sow seed in containers in autumn. Divide in early spring. Slugs and snails may eat the leaves.

Anemonopsis macrophylla

Astelia nervosa

Astelia

Astelia nervosa A plant with attractive foliage that forms tussocks of stiff silvery leaves, to 7ft (2m) long in the wild, although they usually only reach about 2ft (60cm) in gardens in Europe or NW USA. Scented green or reddish flowers are produced in summer. Hardy to 10°F(−12°C), US zones 8–10. Native in New Zealand, growing in moist places in lowland and subalpine forest.

PLANTING HELP For moist peaty or clay soil in shade or partial shade. Water freely in summer and keep moist in winter. Sow seeds when ripe and divide in spring. Protect from frost. Good for gardens in coastal areas.

Astilbe

Astilbe chinensis* var. *pumila A perennial to 18in (45cm) tall, bearing red-green leaves and producing branched spikes of tiny, densely packed reddish-pink flowers in late summer, making excellent ground-cover. The fruiting stems are reddish-brown, attractive in their own right. Hardy to −10°F (−23°C), US zones 6–9. Native to E China.

PLANTING HELP Plant in moist fertile soil in sun or partial shade. Propagate by division when plant is dormant in winter or early spring; should be divided every 4 years or so.

Grasses and Sedges

Grasses and sedges occur all over the world in all types of climate. Some are considered weeds, but many arebeautiful in their own right and make excellent ground cover in shady areas, contrasting well with ferns, and Astilbes.

PLANTING HELP The grasses and sedges illustrated here require fertile, moist, well-drained

Astilbe chinensis var. *pumila*

Carex fraseri

Carex hachijoensis 'Evergold'

Bowles' Golden Grass
Milium effusum 'Aureum'

soil in sun or partial shade. Sow ripe seeds in spring but beware, the variegated forms will not come true from seed. Alternatively, propagate by division in early summer.

Carex fraseri An evergreen perennial which forms dense clumps of stems 6–18in (15 45cm) tall, bearing deep green leaves 1–2in (2.5–5cm) wide. Hardy to 0°F (−18°C), US zones 7–10. Native to eastern North America, growing in moist woods.

***Carex hachijoensis* 'Evergold'** (*C. morrowii* 'Evergold') An evergreen perennial forming dense clumps to 2ft (60cm) wide. Leaves to ½in (1.5cm) wide, with a pale yellowish to white centre. Flowering stems 8–20in (20–50cm). Hardy to 10°F (−12°C), US zones 8–10. Native to woods in Japan.

***Hakonechloa macra* 'Aureola'** A beautiful deciduous grass forming dense clumps of arching stems 15–27in (40–70cm) long. Hardy to 0°F (−18°C), US zones 7–10. Native to Japan, growing on wet cliffs in the mountains.

Bowles' Golden Grass, Wood Millet *Milium effusum* 'Aureum' A perennial grass that forms dense clusters of broad, handsome, freshly coloured leaves and flowers. The stems grow to 3½ft (1m) tall and bear loose clusters of decorative spikes, flowering from May to July. Comes true from seed. Hardy to 0°F (−18°C), US zones 7–10. The green form is found in woodlands in most of Europe.

Mosses

Leucobryum glaucum Mosses are rarely planted in Western gardens, though they may be tolerated or even encouraged. In Japan, however, Moss culture is an important aspect of gardening. They are especially useful in forming neat, slow-growing ground-cover in places where it is too dark for grass to survive. This Moss, made up of individual shoots 8in (20cm) long, forms small humps to 8in (20cm) wide; pale green when fresh, white when dry. Hardy to 0°F (−18°C), US zones 7–10. Native to Europe, growing in open woodland, in acid woods and even on trees in wet areas.

PLANTING HELP For damp soil in shade or a cool position in the open. They require careful treatment; protection from scratching birds and animals and the immediate removal of fallen leaves. Paraquat kills all other green plants, but encourages Mosses.

Moss *Leucobryum glaucum*

A Moss garden in Japan

Lady Fern *Athyrium filix-femina*

Shuttlecock Fern *Matteuccia struthiopteris*

Ferns

Ferns are among the most underrated garden
plants. Used extensively in gardens, and indeed as
house plants during the reign of Queen Victoria,
they have been unfashionable for the past hundred
years or so. Relatively common in the wild, they
provide foliage interest (ferns have no flowers)
from spring through to autumn and are essential
planting for a shady bed.

PLANTING HELP   Most ferns prefer moist,
but not very wet, shade or partial shade. Propagate
either by the spores, common to all ferns, or by
division. Most species are free from pests and
diseases; drought and drying wind are their chief
enemies.

Lady Fern *Athyrium filix-femina*   A deciduous
fern 2–3ft (60–90cm) tall. Hardy to –20°F
(–29°C), US zones 4–8. Widely distributed
throughout Europe, Asia, North Africa and C

North America, growing in deciduous woods on
various, usually acidic soils, but may also be found
in drier and more open habitats. Numerous forms
were brought into cultivation and named in the
19th century, many are still cultivated.

Himalayan Maidenhair Fern *Adiatum venustum*
Although evergreen in temperatures above 10°F
(–12°C), US zones 8–10, this fern is deciduous in
colder conditions. It will spread quite widely, but
not so rapidly as to be troublesome. Fronds 8–12in
(20–30cm) long, are borne on a polished deep
brown stalk 4–6in (10–15cm) long, the new fronds
emerging in early spring. Very hardy and quick to
establish on peat banks or in rock crevices in light
shade or, if not too dry, under trees. Grow in moist
reasonably fertile soil in partial shade. Hardy to
–40°F (–40°C), US zones 3–8. Native to the
Himalayas and W China.

Hart's Tongue, Scolly *Asplenium scolopendrium*
An easily grown perennial fern with bold dramatic

Soft Shield Fern *Polystichum setiferum*

Himalayan Maidenhair Fern *Adiatum venustum*

Soft Tree Fern *Dicksonia antarctica*

Hart's Tongue *Asplenium scolopendrium*

Sensitive Fern *Onoclea sensibilis*

leaves to 24in (60cm) tall, forming clumps as wide as tall. A more stunted form can often be found growing wild in the mortar of old walls; it is quite drought-tolerant once established. Hardy to −20°F (−29°C), US zones 5–9. Native to Europe, Asia and North America. Plant in acid or limy soil with good drainage. Remove old fronds and any leaves that have fallen from overhanging trees to reduce the risk of rust.

Soft Tree Fern *Dicksonia antarctica*
An evergreen tree-fern, usually to 20ft (6m) tall, but it can attain sizes up to 40ft (12m) tall in ideal conditions. Fronds to 13ft (4m) long and 6ft (1.8m) wide, although rarely more than half this size in cultivation. For full or partial shade. Hardy to 10°F (−12°C), US zones 8–10, perhaps more if sheltered. Native to Tasmania and other parts of Australia, in moist forests and along streams. Plant in fertile acid soil, keep moist and fertilize every month, if possible, to encourage large fronds.

Sensitive Fern *Onoclea sensibilis* A deciduous perennial fern that grows up to 2½ft (75cm) tall, spreading to form an extensive colony in good conditions. Hardy to −30°F (−35°C), US zones

4–8. Native to North America and NE Asia growing in wet grassy places, open damp woodland and occasionally on open hillsides. An easily grown fern, spreading quite vigorously when well-estalished in a moist light soil in light shade. The fronds die quickly with the first frosts, providing attractive autumn colour.

Soft Shield Fern *Polystichum setiferum* A hardy and easily grown evergreen fern to 4ft (1.2m) tall. The young unfurling croziers have dense, often silvery scales. Many variations in frond shape have been found, most falling into distinct groups of similar cultivars. Plant in light shade in cool leafy acid or alkaline soil. Hardy to 0°F (−18°C), US zones 7–10. Native to N Europe with similar species in both Asia and North America, growing in deciduous woodland, often in limy soils.

Shuttlecock Fern, Ostrich Plume Fern
Matteuccia struthiopteris A deciduous fern with erect pale green stems 2–4ft (60–120cm) tall, which spread quite rapidly once established. For moist, well-drained leafy soil. Hardy to −40°F (−40°C), US zones 3–8. Native to Europe, Asia and North America in light shade on rocky stream banks, where it may form extensive colonies.

Camass *Camassia leichtlinii*

Cardiocrinum giganteum

Camass

Camassia leichtlinii A bulb which produces stems to 4ft (1.2m) tall with numerous flowers about 1½–3in (4–8cm) wide, opening one at a time in late spring. Hardy to 0°F (–18°C), US zones 7–10. Native to North America. Other *Camassia* species have deep blue flowers.

PLANTING HELP   Plant bulbs about 4in (10cm) deep in autumn in partial shade in moist, fertile, well-drained soil in sun or partial shade. Propagate by removing and planting offsets in summer.

Cardiocrinum

Cardiocrinum giganteum A large bulb producing stems that grow to 12ft (3.5m) tall, bearing scented flowers 9in (23cm) long in summer. Hardy to 0°F (–18°C), US zones 7–10. Native to the Himalayas and W China.

PLANTING HELP   Best planted in late summer or early spring, in moist fertile soil, flourishing in light shade. Protect the young leaves from slugs.

Crocosmia

Crocosmia aurea A perennial with stems to 3½ft (1m) long and different shades of orange flowers, 2in (5cm) across, in early summer. Hardy to 10°F (–12°C), US zones 8–10. Native to South Africa, Malawi, Zambia and Tanzania, growing in woods, along streams in shady gorges, often in conifer plantations.

PLANTING HELP   Plant bulbs in spring, about 4in (10cm) deep, in moist fertile soil in sun or partial soil. Sow seeds when ripe or divide in spring. Needs ample water in summer; can be brought inside and kept dry in winter.

Lilies

Magnificently stately, varied and elegant, lilies will enhance any garden and some tolerate partial shade.

PLANTING HELP   Plant in moist well-drained soil, rich in humus; most Asiatic lilies will tolerate lime or prefer an alkaline soil; and most American species prefer an acid soil rich in peat, moist or even wet, but well drained. As a general rule, place bulb at a depth three times the height of the bulb; most lilies, including *Lilium tigrinum*, produce roots from their stems as well as their bulb and must be planted deep to ensure their roots receive adequate nourishment. For sun or partial shade. Bulbs should be planted in autumn. Insects, small mammals and various fungi and viruses can cause problems.

Lilium martagon
An easily grown plant that grows to 5ft (1.5m)

Lilium martagon

tall, producing clusters of scented flowers which
are usually purplish with black spots but may be
red, pink or white. Hardy to −20°F (−29°C), US
zones 5–9. Native to the Alps, E to the Caucasus.
The most shade-tolerant of all Lilies.

Lilium regale   A beautiful and popular plant
that grows to 5ft (1.5m) tall. The bulb itself is
distinctive, being deep red, and in summer it
produces loose clusters of scented, pure white
flowers with orange anthers that can be up to 5in
(12cm) long. Hardy to −20°F (−29°C), US zones
5–9. Native to China. Needs well-drained limy soil
– even good on rubble.

Lilium lancifolium (syn. *L. tigrinum*)   This
familiar garden lily is long grown in Japan, and
probably originally of hybrid origin. It is very
tolerant of virus, and grows particularly well in
northern gardens in well-drained but rich moist
soil, flowering in August and September. Hardy to
−30°F (−35°C), US zones 4–8.

Lilium 'Citronella'   A fast-growing, clump-
forming plant with clusters of yellow-speckled red
flowers. Hardy to 0°F (−18°C), US zones 7–10.
This lily is derived from various species
originating in Asia.

Tropaeolum

Flame Creeper *Tropaeolum speciosum*
A perennial climber with stems to 16ft (5m) long
and red flowers ¾in (2cm) wide, from summer to
autumn. For a cool shady position in loose peaty
soil. Hardy to 20°F (−6°C), US zones 9–10. Native
to Chile growing in wet forest and scrub.

PLANTING HELP   Plant seeds when ripe and
separate in autumn. May be attacked by
caterpillars or slugs.

Crocosmia aurea

Lilium regale

Lilium lancifolium

Lilium 'Citronella'

Flame Creeper *Tropaeolum speciosum*

'General Schablikine'

Roses

Roses are found growing wild all over the Northern Hemisphere, from the Arctic to North Africa, S India and Mexico, although unknown in the Southern Hemisphere. Their history is complicated and interesting. Rosa gallica was

grown by the Greeks and the Romans, and reintroduced into Europe by the Crusaders returning from the Middle East. Rosa chinensis was bought from China in the 18th century. Many well-known people were avid collectors, not least Empress Josephine of France, wife of Napoleon Bonaparte. Roses have been, and still are, used in cooking, cosmetics, perfumes and medicines.

PLANTING HELP   Most roses prefer to be planted in the sun but these few will tolerate partial shade. Plant in reasonably fertile moist soil, preferably not in a site where roses have recently been grown, in winter or early spring; fertilize regularly for best results. It is important to water frequently in summer to ensure success. Roses are more or less susceptible to many predators and diseases, depending on the individual variety or cultivar.

Rosa glauca (syn. *R. rubrifolia*)   A large shrub to 13ft (4m) tall with arching branches and lovely grey or purplish delicate ornamental foliage and deep purple twigs. Small deep pink flowers with some scent are produced in summer, followed by numerous bright red hips. Found wild in the mountains of Europe from the Pyrenees to Albania. Seems unaffected by disease.

Rose 'Zéphirine Drouhin'

Rosa soulieana A climber to 18ft (5.3m) tall with long slender branches, producing scented flowers, yellow in bud and white on opening, in late summer. The leaves are bluish with rounded leaflets and the fruit is an orange red, oval ½in (1.5cm) long. Native to W China where it grows on rocky hillsides. Discovered by the French missionary Abbé Soulie and sent back to France in 1895.

Rose 'Gloire de Dijon', The Old Glory Rose One of the all-time favourite climbers, to 13ft (4m) tall. Blooms repeatedly throughout the summer. Excellent scent. In warmer weather the pink tones become stronger. Hardy to −20°F (−29°C), US zones 5–9. Raised by Jacotot in France, launched in 1853. Perfectly hardy in England and thrives even on a north wall.

Rose 'General Schablikine' A slightly scented Tea Rose usually reaching to 6ft (1.8m) tall, although it can grow higher if supported. Tea Roses are the result of crossing Chinese wild roses brought to Europe on the tea clippers in the 19th century. Almost never without a flower, this Rose has purple shoots when young, curved flower stalks and is particularly hardy for a Tea Rose. Hardy to 20°F (−6°C), US zones 9–10. Raised by Nabonnand in France, launched 1878.

Rose 'Zéphirine Drouhin' A sweetly scented Bourbon rose that grows to 8ft (2.5m) and 6ft (1.8m) wide with very few thorns, raised by Bizot in France, launched in 1868. Flowers produced continuously from summer through to autumn. Hardy to −20°F (−29°C), US zones 5–9. The best climber for a shady spot. Liable to mildew and blackspot if the root is dry.

'Gloire de Dijon'

Rosa glauca at Hatfield House, Hertfordshire

Rosa soulieana

Rosa glauca

Acer palmatum 'Dissectum Nigrum'

Acer shirasawanum f. *aureum*

Acer palmatum f. *atropurpureum*

Acer

These wonderful trees from Europe, North Africa, Asia and Central and North America are of varying sizes. Some are valued for their exquisitely delicate leaves that turn wonderful shades of red, orange and yellow in the autumn, while others are appreciated for their attractive bark. The smaller trees make truly spectacular garden plants.

PLANTING HELP   Plant in autumn or winter in moist acid

Vine Maple
Acer circinatum

soil, sheltered from the wind. For sun or partial shade. No pruning is necessary except for the removal of dead or damaged wood.

Vine Maple *Acer circinatum*   An elegant deciduous shrub or small tree that grows to 33ft (10m) tall, producing small purple and white flowers in April and May. For shade or partial shade. The tree becomes a magnificent mass of gold in autumn. Hardy to −10°F (−23°C), US zones 6–9. Native to W North America, growing in forests along streams.

Acer palmatum* f. *atropurpureum   A small spreading deciduous tree that grows to about 12ft (3.5m) tall. The reddish-purple leaves become a beautiful vivid red in autumn. Prefers partial shade. Hardy to −20°F (−29°C), US zones 5–9. Native to China, Korea and Japan.

Bamboo *Chusquea couleou*

Acer palmatum 'Dissectum Nigrum'

Moosewood
Acer pennsylvanicum

A low rounded deciduous bush that grows into a mushroom shape about 5ft (1.5m) tall and as wide. The young leaves are covered with silky hairs and the deep reddish-purple colour is retained throughout the summer. Hardy to −20°F (−29°C), US zones 5–9. Native to China, Korea and Japan.

Moosewood *Acer pennsylvanicum* A deciduous shrub or small tree to 35ft (12m) with white striped bark and three-lobed leaves to 7in (18cm) long. Flowers scented, in long catkins in spring. Native to the mountain woods of the Appalachians, from Tennessee north to Quebec. Hardy to −40°F (−40°C), US zones 3–8.

Acer shirasawanum f. *aureum*

(syn. *A. japonicum* 'Aureum') A small shrub or stout tree to 13ft (4m) tall with golden 9–13 pointed leaves and small bunches of red flowers in spring. Native to Japan; the golden form is the one usually seen in gardens. Hardy to −20°F (−29°C), US zones 5–9.

Bamboo

Bamboos are enormous Oriental grasses, although they are very different from common grasses. Previously used as offerings to the gods in Japan, they are still widely utilized in architecture, in the making of furniture and in the production of handicrafts.

PLANTING HELP   For moist rich soil in shelter and partial shade. Keep young plants moist until well-established. Divide or separate rhizomes in spring. Young shoots of *Sasa palmata* and *Fargesia murieliae* may be eaten by slugs. Many bamboos will spread quickly and will need to have the new growth contained to avoid them taking over the garden.

Pleioblastus viridistriatus (syn. *P. auricomus*) A plant that forms wide mats of stems 5ft (1.5m) long, bearing downy golden leaves 7 × 1in (18 × 2.5cm). For sun or partial shade. Hardy to 0°F (−18°C), US zones 7–10. Native to forests of Japan.

Chusquea culeou One of the few hardy South American bamboos, an evergreen forming clumps of arching stems 13–20ft (4–6m) tall, with short nodes. For sun or light shade. Hardy to 0°F (−18°C), US zones 7–10. Native to forests of Chile and S Argentina.

Pleioblastus viridistriatus

85

Fuchsia 'Riccartonii'

Fuchsia

Deciduous or evergreen shrubs or small trees
from Central and South America and New
Zealand. Many thousands of cultivars have been
raised; in fact, most garden plants are of hybrid
origin. The flowers, in pinks, reds, purples and
whites are dainty and pendulous, rather
reminiscent of children dressed up as fairies!
Fuchsias make excellent planting companions for
spring bulbs because they do not start growing
until late spring.

PLANTING HELP   Plant in autumn or early
spring in any moist soil in sun or shade, preferably
not under trees. Place plants approximately 2in
(5cm) deep and mulch in winter, protecting roots

Fuchsia magellanica var.
   molinae 'Sharpitor'

in cold areas. Sow seed or root cuttings indoors in
spring. Insects may cause problems.

***Fuchsia magellanica* var. *molinae*
'Sharpitor'**   The hardiest of the fuchsias, this
cultivar has a very light pink, almost white outside
(sepal) enclosing pale lavender petals and pink
insides (stamens). The leaves are of the palest
green, edged with creamy white. Hardy to 0°F
(−18°C), US zones 7–10. 'Sharpitor' is a sport
from *Fuchsia magellanica* var. *molinae*, which is
native to Chile. First noticed at Overbecks
(Sharpitor), a National Trust garden at Salcombe,
Devon, England. Less vigorous than *Fuchsia
magellanica* var. *molinae*, it looks wonderful when
planted with colchicums.

***Fuchsia* 'Riccartonii'**   A vigorous deciduous
shrub that grows to 6ft (1.8m) tall, producing
flowers 1in (2.5cm) long in summer. The narrowly
oval leaves are about 1½ in (4cm) long and the
fruit is an oblong berry ¾in (2cm) long, black
when ripe. Hardy to 10°F (−12°C), US zones 8–10
or even lower when established. Raised in
Scotland in the 19th century, 'Riccartonii' is
believed to be a variant of *Fuchsia magellanica*. It is
one of the less hardy forms of this species and may
need some protection in cold areas. This is the
variety which forms spectacular hedges along the
west coast of Ireland.

Mitraria

Mitraria coccinea An evergreen climber or
scrambling shrub that grows to 10ft (3m) or more.
Hairy leaves ¾in (2cm) long and flowers 1–1½in
(2.5–4cm). Hardy to 10°F (–12°C), US zones
8–10. Native to southern South America, growing
on moss-covered tree trunks and rocks in deep
shade in forests.

PLANTING HELP Plant in moist, fertile,
lime-free soil in partial shade and shelter. Sow
seed indoors in spring or root cuttings in summer.
Shelter from cold winds.

Mitraria coccinea

Hypericum 'Hidcote'

St John's Wort

Hypericums are deciduous evergreen and
semi-evergreen shrubs and trees, annuals and
perennials from a wide range of habitats. Their
cup-shaped yellow flowers add interest to the
garden in late summer and early autumn, some
have leaves with attractive autumn colour, others
ornamental fruits.

PLANTING HELP For any good soil in sun or
partial shade, although a few will thrive in deep
shade; *Hypericum calycinum*, which is a parent of
Hypericum 'Hidcote', is such an example. Divide
perennials in late spring and reshape bush in
spring or autumn if required; plants are sometimes
partially killed back in the winter and the damaged
stems should be pruned out in the early spring.
Perennials can be afflicted by a rust disease.

Hypericum '**Hidcote**' A compact semi-
evergreen shrub that grows to 6ft (1.8m) tall and
as wide, producing clusters of flowers, each about
3in (8cm) wide, over a long period
in the summer. The leaves
are 2–3in (5–8cm) long.
Hardy to –10°F
(–23°C), US zones
6–9. Very showy in
flower, this has
become one of the
most frequently
planted hardy
shrubs. Thought to
be a hybrid between
Hypericum calycinum and
one of the Chinese species.

Hypericum kouytchense
(syns. *Hypericum patulum* var.
grandiflorum, *Hypericum*
'Sungold')
A semi-evergeen
shrub to 5ft (1.5m)
tall. Drooping
branches bear short-
stalked dark bluish-
green leaves 2in (5cm)
long, and produce
flowers 2½in (6cm)
wide. Hardy to 10°F
(–12°C), US zones
8–10. Native to
China.

Hypericum kouytchense

Hydrangea aspera
'Villosa'

Hydrangeas

Hydrangeas are a genus of deciduous or evergreen shrubs and climbers from the woods of Asia and America, grown primarily for their magnificent flower heads. The bark of some varieties is very attractive in mature plants, many bear handsome foliage and others exhibit sensational autumn colour. The flower colour is affected by the alkalinity of the soil; acid soils produce blue flowers, whereas neutral to alkaline soils produce pink flowers; it is possible to introduce a blueing agent, like aluminium sulphate to the soil if it is neutral. However, there are white-flowered varieties whose colour is unaffected by the soil.

PLANTING HELP   Plant in moist, reasonably fertile soil in sun or partial shade and shelter from

cold winds. It is important to ensure that smaller plants are well watered in summer or they may not fulfil their flowering potential. Root softwood cuttings in summer and hardwood cuttings in winter. Can be attacked by insects and mould, and often damaged by late frosts.

***Hydrangea aspera* Villosa Group** (syn. *H. aspera* subsp. *aspera*)   A large deciduous shrub that grows to 12ft (3.5m) tall and usually wider, bearing hairy leaves 8in (20cm) long, and producing broad flat clusters of small lilac pink fertile flowers, each about ¾in (2cm) wide, in late summer and autumn. Hardy to 0°F (−18°C), US zones 7–10. Native to the Himalayas, China and Taiwan. Plants forming the Villosa group came from China early in the 20th century. They make magnificent specimens, more compact than *Hydrangea aspera* itself, and can be the focus of interest in the early autumn, doing particularly well against a north-facing wall. Very lime-tolerant.

Hydrangea aspera* subsp. *sargentiana (syn. *Hydrangea sargentiana*)   A deciduous shrub that grows to 7ft (2m) tall or more, often gaunt in cultivation, producing sterile white or pink flowers in a head to 8in (20cm) wide in late summer. Hardy to 0°F (−18°C), US zones 7–10. Native to scrub in China.

***Hydrangea macrophylla* 'Veitchii'** A deciduous lacecap hydrangea, so-called because of the flat-topped white flower heads consisting of tiny fertile flowers surrounded by larger sterile flowers; their colour becomes pink and eventually red as they age. To 5ft (1.5m) tall and hardy to 0°F (−18°C), US zones 7–10. A cultivar of *Hydrangea macrophylla* (Common Hydrangea), introduced at the beginning of the 20th century from Japan.

Climbing Hydrangea *Hydrangea petiolaris* (*H. anomala* subsp. *petiolaris*)   A deciduous shrub that grows to 60ft (18m) tall, even more in the wild. Produces large flat clusters of small creamy white flowers surrounded by showier florets, as much as 9in (23cm) wide, in midsummer; the flowers are produced more freely on mature plants. Hardy to −10°F (−23°C), US zones 6–9. Native to Russia, Korea, Taiwan and Japan. A magnificent large climber for a shady wall.

Hydrangea serrata A deciduous lacecap hydrangea with small leaves and delicate pink or blue flowers in heads around 6in (15cm) across, smaller than 'Veitchii'. Hardy to 0°F (−18°C), US zones 7–10. Native to mountain woods in Japan. 'Bluebird' is a good cultivar.

Hydrangea macrophylla 'Veitchii'

Hydrangea aspera subsp. *sargentiana*

Hydrangea serrata

Climbing Hydrangea *Hydrangea petiolaris*

Colchicum speciosum 'Album'

Naked Ladies *Colchicum speciosum*

Wild Cyclamen *Cyclamen hederifolium*

Autumn Crocus

Naked Ladies *Colchicum speciosum*   A member of
the lily family which produces large bright pink,
often white-throated, crocus-like flowers up to 7in
(18cm) tall and 4in (10cm) wide, as autumn
begins. The flowers arrive without foliage or
indeed any stem, and the leaves, which are
poisonous, do not appear until early spring. Native
of the mountains of northern Turkey in alpine
meadows. Like many colchicums, *Colchicum
speciosum* can become naturalized in grass, and
will flower in light shade.
Colchicum speciosum 'Album'   White goblet
crocus-like flowers with exceptional purity of
colour, up to 5in (12cm) tall.

PLANTING HELP   Easily grown from bulbs
which will multiply over the years to form
attractive clumps. Plant bulbs approximately 4in
(10cm) deep in summer or at the beginning of
autumn, in moist, fertile, well-drained soil in sun
or partial shade. Contact with skin may cause
irritation.

Cyclamen

Wild Cyclamen *Cyclamen hederifolium* (syn.
C. neapolitanum)   A corm that grows to 3in (8cm)
wide, producing flowers about 1in (2.5cm) long in
early autumn. The plants are dormant in summer
and need little water then, unless earlier flowering
is required. Hardy to −10°F (−23°C), US zones
6–9. Native to the Mediterranean and W Asia.

PLANTING HELP   Plant corm approximately
2in (5cm) deep in sun or partial shade. Sow
soaked and washed seed in darkness as soon as
ripe. Beware, small animals sometimes dig up the
corms.

Disanthus

Disanthus cercidifolius   A large deciduous
shrub or small multi-stemmed tree to 15ft (4.5m)
tall, grown entirely for its foliage. The leaves 3–5in
(8–12cm) wide, turn to very striking red, purple
and sometimes orange tints before falling in late
autumn, when pairs of inconspicuous maroon
flowers with a slight but unpleasant scent, are
produced. Hardy to 0°F (−18°C), US zones 7–10.
Native to southern Japan where it is found
growing in damp woodland.

PLANTING HELP   Plant in acid or neutral
soil in a sheltered, partially shaded position in
autumn or early spring, ideally under the canopy
of tall trees.

Disanthus cercidifolius

Photinia

Photinia davidiana (syn. *Stranvaesia davidiana*)
A large evergreen shrub that grows to 33ft (10m)
tall with erect branches and spreading side shoots.
The olive green leathery leaves 2¼–4in (6–10cm)
long, contrast beautifully with the white flowers
which are followed by drooping clusters of bright
crimson fruits. These usually last until the New
Year when the leaves become scarlet. Native to W
China, south to Vietnam.
Photinia davidiana* var. *undulata (*illustrated
here*) has smaller shinier leaves and a spreading
habit. Hardy to 10°F (–12°C), US zones 8–10.

PLANTING HELP   Plant in any well-drained
soil in sun or partial shade and some shelter. No
pruning is required, but it can spread widely
unless restricted. Propagate from seed or summer
cuttings.

Photinia davidiana
var. *undulata*

Hamamelis 'Arnold Promise' (*see page 17 for text*) is
one of the best shrubs for autumn colour

Vitis

Vitis coignetiae   A magnificent deciduous
climbing shrub that grows to 80ft (24m) tall, given
suitable support; best grown on a long stretch of
fence or up into a tall tree. In early summer it
bears inconspicuous clusters of small greenish-
yellow flowers. The handsome, prominently veined
leaves to 12ft (3.5m) long, are covered with a fawn
felt on the underside and turn to brilliant shades
of orange and red in autumn. The fruit is an edible
purple black berry about 1½in (4cm) across, but is
not freely produced. Hardy to –10°F (–23°C), US
zones 6–9. Native to Japan and Korea

PLANTING HELP   Plant in autumn or spring
in any soil, in sun or partial shade. No regular
pruning is required, other than to control its
spread.

Vitis coignetiae climbing into Mongolian Lime trees, in northern Hokkaido, Japan

Fatsia japonica

Fatsia japonica 'Variegata'

Common Ivy *Hedera helix*

Fatsia

Japanese Aralia *Fatsia japonica*   A large evergreen shrub that grows to 12ft (3.5m) tall and usually wider. In late autumn it produces branched clusters of circular white flower heads composed of many tiny flowers, each about 2½in (6cm) wide. The long-stalked leathery leaves are 12in (30cm) wide and the pea-sized fruit is black when ripe. Hardy to 10°F (−12°C), US zones 8–10. Native to S Japan and particularly appropriate to town gardens where its handsome foliage makes a bold statement against walls.

***Fatsia japonica* 'Variegata'** Leaves broadly edged with cream.

PLANTING HELP
Any soil in shelter and shade. Water freely in spring and summer. Propagate from cuttings.

Ivy

Ivies are evergreen climbers and creepers which cling to their supports. They vary enormously in size and vigour, and are native to light woodland habitats. Ideal for covering a shady wall or as ground-cover; pinning the young stems will encourage them to cling.

Irish Ivy
Hedera hibernica

PLANTING HELP   Ivies will thrive in quite deep shade but are best protected from cold winds. Although tolerant of most soils, rich fertile soils will produce a more luxuriant foliage; mulch in autumn and spring and fertilize in spring for the best results. Propagate by cuttings or by layering in summer. Water freely in summer. Insects and leaf spot may cause problems.

Common Ivy, **English Ivy** *Hedera helix*
An evergreen shrub with glossy leaves usually less than 6in (15cm) long. Creeping or climbing to 100ft (30m) tall in its juvenile stage, it becomes shrubby with less lobed leaves and flowers in the adult stage. Greenish flowers are produced in September and October and are much visited by flies, bees and butterflies for late nectar. The black fruit usually ripens in spring. Hardy to −10°F (−23°C), US zones 6–9. Native to most of Europe except the far north, east to Turkey and the Caucasus, climbing on trees, rocks and walls.

Irish Ivy *Hedera hibernica* (syn. *Hedera helix* subsp. *hibernica*)   Growing rapidly to 30ft (9m) tall, this ivy produces dark green leaves 2–3in (5–8cm) long with five star-shaped lobes. Hardy to 0°F (−18°C), US zones 7–10. Native to W Europe, in sheltered places usually near the coast.

Holly

Hollies are a diverse group of evergreen and deciduous shrubs which will thrive in sun or partial shade, and are excellent for hedging; most garden varieties are evergreen. Male and female flowers are usually borne on separate plants and both are needed in order to produce berries.

PLANTING HELP   Plant in autumn or spring in partial shade, but avoid wet weather. *Ilex aquifolium* can be raised from seed and self-seeds quite freely but the seedlings grow extremely slowly at first. Prune holly hedges in spring; they will tolerate quite radical pruning. Other hollies can be cut back in summer. Mulch in autumn and early spring and fertilize in spring. Propagation is extremely difficult. Young shoots are susceptible to insects.

Ilex aquifolium   An evergreen shrub or tree to 55ft (16m) tall , bearing stiff wavy edged leaves usually with spines, at least on lower branches, and shiny dark green above. Fruits ¼–⅓ in (0.5–1cm). Hardy to 0°F (−18°C), US zones 7–10, for short periods. Native to W Europe, eastwards to Austria, S Turkey and N Iran, in woods, hedges and on cliffs, usually on acid soils.

Golden King Holly *Ilex* × *altaclerensis* 'Golden King'   An attractive, golden-variegated evergreen that can grow to 40ft (12m) tall or more. Each small white female flower is about ¼in (0.5cm) wide. The oval leaves are 2–4in (5–10cm) long. In spite of its name, this plant is female and produces red berries in winter. Hardy to 0°F (−18°C), US zones 7–10. A female sport of *Ilex* × *altaclerensis* 'Hendersonii'.

Holly
Ilex aquifolium

Golden King Holly

INDEX

Index

Acer
  circinatum 84
  japonicum 'Aureum' 84
  palmatum
    'Dissectum Nigrum' 84
    f. atropurpureum 84
  pennsylvanicum 85
  shirasawanum f. aureum 84
Actaea
  erythrocarpa 27
  rubra f. neglecta 27
Adiatum venustum 78
Ajuga reptans 9
Alchemilla mollis 74
Allium
  triquetrum 38
  ursinum 38
Amberbell 36
American Columbine 32
Anemone
  flaccida 19
  nemorosa 13
  rivularis 19
Anemonella thalictroides f. rosea 19
Anemonopsis macrophylla 75
Aquilegia
  'Hensol Harebell' 32
  canadensis 32
  vulgaris 32
Arisaema sikokianum 39
Arum italicum 'Pictum' 38
  'Marmoratum' 38
Asarina procumbens 75
Asperula odorata 72
Asplenium scolopendrium 79
Astelia nervosa 76
Astilbe chinensis var pumila 76
Athyrium filix-femina 78
Aucuba japonica 'Variegata' 46
Autumn Crocus 90

Bamboo 85
Baneberry 27
Barrenwort 24
Bear's Garlic 38
Beetleweed 64
Bergenia
  'Baby Doll' 18
  'Bressingham White' 18
  cordifolia 18
Birthroot 38
Bishop's Mitre 24
Bleeding Heart 25
Blue Bells 30
Bluebell 36
Bowles' Golden Grass 76
Box 46
Boxwood 46
Brunnera macrophylla 30
  'Hadspen Cream' 30
Bugle 9
Bunchberry 74
Buxus sempervirens 46

Buxus sempervirens (Cont.)
  'Aureovariegata' 46
  'Latifolia Maculata' 46

Camass 80
Camassia leichtlinii 80
Camellia
  'Cornish Snow' 42
  japonica 42
    'Adolphe Audusson' 43
    'Adolphe Audusson Variegated'
                                42
    'Akashigata' 42
    'Juno' 42
    'Jupiter' 42
    'Lady Clare' 42
    'Lavinia Maggi' 42
    'Mathotiana Rosea' 43
    'Sylvia' 42
    'Tricolor' 43
  sasanqua 40
    'Hebe' 40
    'Hugh Evans' 40
    'Mine-no-yuki' 40
    'Narumigata' 40
    'White Dove' 40
  × williamsii 41
    'Anticipation' 41
    'Bow Bells' 41
    'E. G. Waterhouse' 40
    'Jury's Yellow' 41
Campanula
  latifolia 72
  takesimana 72
Candelabra Primula 28
Cardamine
  heptaphylla 22
  pentaphyllos 22
Cardiocrinum giganteum 80
Carex
  fraseri 76
  hachijoensis 'Evergold' 76
Caucasian Comfrey 20
Chamaepericlymenum
                canadense 74
Chinese Pieris 45
Chinese Witch Hazel 17
Chionodoxa species 11
Christmas Rose 6
Chusquea couleou 85
Cimicifuga rubifolia 64
Climbing Hydrangea 89
Colchicum
  speciosum 90
  'Album' 90
Common Foxglove 73
Common Ivy 92
Convallaria majalis 57
Cornus
  canadensis 74
  florida 54
Correa
  'Harrisii' 14
  'Mannii' 14
Corsican Hellebore 7
Corydalis

Corydalis (Cont.)
  flexuosa 'China Blue' 58
  lutea 58
  ochroleuca 58
Corylopsis sinensis
    'Spring Purple' 45
    'Veitchiana' 45
  var. sinensis 44
Cowslip 23
Cranesbill 59
Creeping Jenny 64
Crocosmia aurea 81
Cyclamen
  atkinsii 12
  coum 12
  hederifolium 90
  neapolitanum 90
  orbiculatum 12

Dame's Violet 26
Daphne
  laureola 16
  odora 16
    'Aureomarginata' 16
    'Marginata' 16
  retusa 16
  tangutica retusa group 16
Dentaria
  digitata 22
  pentaphyllos 22
  pinnata 22
Dianella tasmanica 56
Dicentra
  formosa subsp. oregona
                'Langtrees' 25
  spectabilis 25
Dicksonia antarctica 79
Digitalis purpurea 73
Diphylleia cymosa 34
Disanthus cercidifolius 90
Disporum sessile 'Variegatum' 56
Dog's Tooth Violet 36
Dondia epipactis 34
Doronicum
  caucasicum 65
  orientale 65
  pardalianches 65
Dusky Cranesbill 59

Endymion non-scriptus 36
English Ivy 92
English Violet 33
Eomecon chionantha 60
Epimedium
  grandiflorum 24
  macranthum 24
  pinnatum 24
  × rubrum 24
  × versicolor 'Sulphureum' 24
Eranthis hyemalis 11
Erythronium
  dens-canis 36
    'Pagoda' 37
  americanum 36
Euonymus japonicus 46
Euphorbia

INDEX

Euphorbia *(Cont.)*
  amygdaloides 23
  griffithii 23

Fairy Bells 56
Fatsia japonica 92
Flame Creeper 81
Flowering Dogwood 54
Foam Flower 62
Forget-me-not 31
Foxglove 73
Fuchsia
  'Riccartonii' 86
  magellanica var. molinae
  'Sharpitor' 86

Galanthus nivalis 10
Galax
  aphylla 64
  urceolata 64
Galium odoratum 72
Gentiana asclepiadea 72
Geranium
  endressii 59
  nodosum 59
  phaeum 59
  sylvaticum 59
Glory of the Snow 11
Granny's Bonnet 32
Great Leopard's Bane 65
Guelder Rose 55

Hacquetia epipactis 34
Hakonechloa macra 'Aureola' 77
Halesia monticola 55
Hamamelis
  mollis 17
  × intermedia
    'Arnold Promise' 17, 91
    'Jelena' 17
Hart's Tongue 79
Hedera
  helix 92
  hibernica 92
    subsp. hibernica 92
Helleborus
  argutifolius 7
  corsicus 7
  foetidus 6
  lividus subsp. corsicus 7
  niger 6
  orientalis 6
    'Atrorubens' 7
    'Celadon' 7
    'Cosmos' 7
  purpurascens 6
Hesperis matronalis 26
Heuchera
  'Palace Purple' 63
  cylindrica 63
  'Greenfinch' 63
Himalayan Maidenhair Fern 78
Himalayan Blue Poppy 61
Holly 93
  Golden King 93
Honesty 26

Horned Pansy 33
Hosta
  'August Moon' 71
  'Ginko Craig' 69
  'Gold Edger' 70
  'Gold Standard' 70
  'Halcyon' 66
  'Honeybells' 70
  'Krossa Regal' 67
  'Royal Standard' 66
  'Shade Fanfare' 69
  'Thomas Hogg' 69
  'Wayside Perfection' 66
  'Wide Brim' 70
  'Zounds' 71
  fortunei 'Aureo-marginata' 68
  sibthorpii 29
  sieboldiana 66
    'Frances Williams' 66
  undulata
    'Albomarginata' 69
    var. univittata 68
  ventricosa 69
    'Aureomaculata' 69
    'Maculata' 69
  vulgaris 29
    subsp. sibthorpii 29
  whitei 'Sherriff's Variety' 28
Houttuynia
  cordata 75
  'Variegata' 75
Hyacinthoides non-scripta 36
Hydrangea
  anomala subsp. petiolaris 89
  aspera
    subsp. aspera 88
    subsp. sargentiana 89
    Villosa Group 88
  macrophylla 'Veitchii' 88
  petiolaris 89
  sargentiana 89
  serrata 89
Hypericum
  'Hidcote' 87
  'Sungold' 87
  kouytchense 87
  patulum var. grandiflorum 87

Ilex
  aquifolium 93
  × altaclerensis 'Golden King' 93
Iris 'Katharine Hodgkin' 13
Irish Ivy 92
Ivy 92

Japanese Aralia 92
Jeffersonia dubia 34
Jerusalem Cowslip 21

Kingcup 23

Lady Fern 78
Lady's Mantle 74
Lamium
  galeobdolon 'Florentinum' 9
  maculatum 9

Lamium *(Cont.)*
  'Roseum' 9
  'White Nancy' 9
Large Merrybells 35
Lenten Rose 6
Leopard's Bane 65
Lesser Periwinkle 8
Leucobryum glaucum 77
Lily 80
Lilium
  'Citronella' 81
  lancifolium 81
  martagon 80
  regale 81
  tigrinum 81
Lily-of-the-valley 57
Liriope muscari 57
Lunaria
  annua 26
  rediviva 27
Lysimachia nummularia 'Aurea' 64

Magnolia
  sieboldii subsp. sinensis 48
  soulangeana 'Rustica Rubra' 48
  stellata 49
  wilsonii 49
  × loebneri 'Leonard Messel' 48
Mahonia
  aquifolium 15
  japonica 15
  × media 'Charity' 15
Marsh Marigold 23
Matteuccia struthiopteris 78
Meconopsis
  baileyi 61
  betonicifolia 61
  cambrica 61
  grandis 60
  quintuplinervia 61
  villosa 61
Mertensia
  pulmonarioides 30
  virginica 30
Milium effusum 'Aureum' 76
Mitella breweri 62
Mitraria coccinea 87
Moneywort 64
Moosewood 85
Moss 77
Mountain Snowdrop Tree 55
Mourning Widow 59
Myosotis sylvatica 31.

Naked Ladies 90
Nectaroscordum siculum 37
New Zealand Mountain Foxglove 23
Omphalodes cappadocica
    'Cherry Ingram' 21
Onoclea sensibilis 79
Oregon Grape 15
Ostrich Plume Fern 78
Ourisia macrophylla 23
Oxalis acetosella 35
Oxlip 28

INDEX

Pachyphragma macrophyllum 27
Perennial Honesty 27
Photinia davidiana 91
  × fraseri 'Robusta' 46
Pick-a-back plant 62
Pieris
  'Forest Flame' 45
  formosa var. forrestii 45
Plagiorhegma dubia 34
Platycodon grandiflorus 72
Pleioblastus
  auricomus 85
  viridistriatus 85
Podophyllum hexandrum 35
Polystichum setiferum 78
Primrose 29
Primula
  bhutanica 28
  elatior 28
  flaccida 28
  helodoxa 28
  nutans 28
  prolifera 28
Pseudofumaria alba 58
Pulmonaria
  angustifolia 21
  officinalis 21
  rubra 'Redstart' 21

Ramsons 38
Ranunculus
  ficaria 12
  'Brazen Hussy' 12
Rhododendron
  'Blaue Donau' 53
  'Blue Danube' 53
  'Cilpinense' 50
  'Elizabeth' 51
  'Hershey's Red' 53
  'Narcissiflora' 52
  'Purple Splendour' 51
  'Temple Belle' 50
  'Vuyk's Scarlet' 52
  dauricum
    'Midwinter' 53
  fulvum 51
  lutescens 51
  schlippenbachii 53

Rhododendron *(Cont.)*
  yakushimanum 51
Rosa
  glauca 83
  rubrifolia 83
  soulieana 83
Rose
  'General Schablikine' 82
  'Gloire de Dijon' 83
  'Zéphirine Drouhin' 82
Running-myrtle 8

Satin Flower 26
Saxifraga fortunei 63
Saxifrage 63
Scolly 79
Sensitive Fern 79
Shuttlecock Fern 78
Silphium perfoliatum 65
Skimmia japonica 47
  'Rubella' 47
Snowdrop 10
Soft Shield Fern 78
Soft Tree Fern 79
Soldiers and Sailors 21
Spotted Dog 21
Spurge 22
Spurge Laurel 16
St John's Wort 87
Star Magnolia 49
Stinking Hellebore 6
Stranvaesia davidiana 91
Sweet Violet 33
Sweet White Violet 33
Sweet Woodruff 72
Symphytum
  caucasicum 20
  orientale 20
Synthyris missurica 74
Synthyris *(Cont.)*
  stellata 74

Three-cornered Leek 38
Tiarella cordifolia 62
Toad Lilies 56
Tolmiea menziesii 62
Toothwort 22
Tricyrtis hirta 56

Trillium grandiflorum 38
Tropaeolum speciosum 81
Trout Lily 36

Umbrella Leaf 34
Uvularia grandiflora 35
Variegated Comfrey 20

Viburnum
  × bodnantense 'Dawn' 14
  opulus 'Sterile' 55
  plicatum 'Mariesii' 55
Vinca
  difformis 8
  minor 8
    'Argenteovariegata' 8
    'Atropurpurea' 8
Vine Maple 84
Viola 33
  blanda 33
  cornuta 33
  odorata 33
Virginia Cowslip 30
Vitis coignetiae 91

Wake Robin 38
Weigela florida 'Foliis Purpureis' 54
Welsh Poppy 61
White Comfrey 20
Wild Cyclamen 90
Wild Hyacinth 36
Willow Gentian 72
Wilson's Magnolia 49
Windflower 13
Winter Aconite 11
Winter Daphne 16
Wood Anemone 13
Wood Cranesbill 59
Wood Garlic 38
Wood Lily 38
Wood Millet 76
Wood Sorrel 35
Woodspurge 23

Yellow Adder's Tongue 36
Youth-on-age 62

Zantedeschia aethiopica 39